KEEPING FAITH

KEEPING FAITH

Embracing the Tensions in Christian Higher Education

Essays and Pieces on the Occasion of the Inauguration of Gaylen J. Byker as President of Calvin College

Edited by

Ronald A. Wells

William B. Eerdmans Publishing Company
Grand Rapids, Michigan / Cambridge, U.K.

© 1996 Wm. B. Eerdmans Publishing Co.
255 Jefferson Ave. S.E., Grand Rapids, Michigan 49503 /
P.O. Box 163, Cambridge CB3 9PU U.K.

Printed in the United States of America

01 00 99 98 97 96   7 6 5 4 3 2 1

Library of Congress Cataloging-in-Publication Data

Keeping faith : embracing the tensions in Christian higher
education : essays and pieces on the occasion of the inauguration
of Gaylen J. Byker as president of Calvin College /
edited by Ronald A. Wells.
p.   cm.
ISBN 0-8028-4238-0 (alk. paper)
1. Christian education. 2. Church and education.
3. Church colleges. 4. Calvin College.
I. Wells, Ronald, 1941-   . II. Byker, Gaylen, J.
BV1473.K39 1996
377'.842 — dc20   96-9147
CIP

Contents

Introduction   vii
    Ronald A. Wells

The Maturity Mandate: A Sermon   1
    Richard J. Mouw

Dream of the School   8
    Lionel Basney

The Embarrassment of Riches   11
    Gaylen J. Byker

Piety and Progress: A History of Calvin College   20
    James D. Bratt and Ronald A. Wells

"Once More Unto the Breach, Dear Friends":
Gender Studies and the Christian Academy   47
    Susan Van Zanten Gallagher

v

The Supreme Court, Societal Elites, and Calvin College:
Christian Higher Education in a Secular Age   67
   Stephen V. Monsma

"Dutch" and Reformed and "Black" and Reformed
in South Africa: A Tale of Two Traditions on the
Move to Unity and Responsibility   85
   Russel Botman

"You Talkin' to Me?": The Christian Liberal Arts
Tradition and the Challenge of Popular Culture   106
   William D. Romanowski

Should the Work of Our Hands Have Standing
in the Christian College?   133
   Nicholas P. Wolterstorff

Notes on Contributors   152

Introduction

In 1995, the community of scholars, administrators, trustees, staff, students, and alumni of Calvin College experienced the rare opportunity of inaugurating a new president. It afforded a chance for reflection and renewal. This book is the permanent record of those two days in the autumn of 1995 when people connected with Calvin College joined in minds and spirits to introduce — and be introduced to — Gaylen J. Byker, the eighth president of Calvin College.

The Inaugural Steering Committee, chaired by Gordon L. Van Harn, Senior Vice-President and Provost, was convinced that the inauguration should be characterized by both dignified pomp and circumstance and celebration of the college's past and future. One feature that was to distinguish this inaugural from most others in North American academic culture was the desire of the committee, endorsed by president-elect Byker, to have lectures in the afternoon, following the inauguration ceremony in the morning and a campus-wide lunch at midday. I was given the task of conceiving of and organizing the lectures. I was aided by a subcommittee. We decided several things: that the lectures should, in some significant ways, draft off the theme that had been established for the whole inauguration, "Keeping Faith: Embracing the Tensions"; and that the lectures should address questions of significance not only for Calvin College but also for Christian education and Christian living.

The seven lecturers were chosen because of their distinguished prior records of advocating the Christian cause in publications and in public presentations. While this is not the place to try to summarize the essays printed below, I can venture a few generalizations. There is little, if any, conventional wisdom here. The writers were unafraid to be revisionist in their various areas of concern. They were encouraged by early draft reports of Dr. Byker's address that this Inauguration Day was not likely to be conventional. Byker's address demonstrates his own commitment to being unafraid of where ideas would lead. Whether in reconstructing the history of the college, in discussing race relations, in advocating gender equity, in taking on the challenge of popular culture, in seeking a Christian social stance, or in relating social Christianity to life, these essays probe issues that are, at the same time, vitally important for celebrating Calvin College, but also for charting its course for the future. Moreover, the issues raised here are very important to the life and work of other North American institutions of higher education.

When the book was being brought together for publication, we decided to go beyond the lecturers and the inaugural address by the new president. The sermon by President Mouw and the poem by Professor Basney were worthy complements to the other pieces of this work. We print them in the same chronology of their presentation. Finally, we have two hopes for this book: that it might be an enduring record of what was said on October 29-30, 1995, and that it might be a challenge for Christians everywhere to eschew a shallow consensus on the deep questions, but rather to develop, with the confidence that God gives us, a world-and-life view that answers to the realities of the dynamically changing world of the twenty-first century.

Ronald A. Wells

The Maturity Mandate: A Sermon

Richard J. Mouw

. . . until all of us come to the unity of the faith and of the knowledge of the Son of God, to maturity, to the measure of the full stature of Christ.

Ephesians 4:13

I heard a report a while back about a minister in a denomination that has been plagued in recent years by much infighting. Whenever this minister is present in a gathering where he is convinced that the arguing has gone on too long, he stands up and makes this brief speech: "The *main* thing is to see to it that the *main thing* is the main *thing!*"

The installation of a new president at Calvin College is clearly an occasion where it is important to focus on "the main thing," to reflect together on what this business of Christian liberal arts education is all about. Our text from Ephesians 4 is one of those wonderful main-thing passages in the Scriptures. Here the apostle lists the gifts that the Lord has given to the Christian community. It is especially fitting to point out on this significant occasion that teaching is one of the gifts that he mentions. But it is also important to attend to the job description that the apostle connects to the exercise of these gifts: we must equip God's people for service in such a way that we may all "come to the unity of the faith and of

1

the knowledge of the Son of God, to maturity, to the full stature of Christ" (Eph. 4:12-13).

Here, then, is an important mandate for those who are called to give leadership in Christian liberal arts education. *Aim at maturity*. Educate in such a way that people will move toward attaining the measure of the full stature of Christ.

It is important for us to be very explicit on a regular basis — certainly on milestone occasions like this one — that the goal that we are seeking to promote in Christian higher education is indeed a more mature awareness of who Jesus Christ is. This has certainly been the central aim of Calvin College throughout its history. Calvin's academic leaders have been very conscious of a strong tendency, both in the tradition of spirituality that has shaped our particular strand of Dutch Calvinism and in the spiritual proclivities of our closest evangelical kinfolk, to see growth in Christ primarily in intensive terms: Getting to know Jesus better is often thought of in terms of experiencing an increasingly intense closeness to the Son of God. This spirituality, even in its distortions and excesses, has much to commend it. But the Calvin community has always insisted that the emphasis on intensive growth must be integrated with an equally strong commitment to extensive growth: Getting to know Jesus better also means growing in our awareness of the extent of his power and authority.

At its best, the kind of Dutch Calvinism that has shaped the Calvin College ethos has integrated these emphases together well in a kind of creative tension. Indeed, it has held them together under a common motif of *ownership and belonging*. The intensity of a personal faith has been beautifully expressed in those words of the Heidelberg Catechism, words that many Dutch Calvinists have quoted as they have passed into eternity: that "my only comfort in life and death" is "that I, with body and soul, both in life and death, am not my own, but belong unto my faithful Savior Jesus Christ, who with his precious blood has fully satisfied for all my sins. . . ." But this testimony to our very personal sense of belonging to Jesus has been regularly coupled on this campus with another profound manifesto that itself has come to have a kind of catechetical status among us: Abraham Kuyper's bold proclamation that "there is not one square inch of the entire creation about which Jesus Christ does not say, 'This is mine! This belongs to me!' "

That is a powerful combination of emphases: I belong to Jesus; and the whole cosmos, in all of its created complexity, also belongs to him. It is of crucial importance for the kind of liberal arts education to which this community is committed that they be kept together. And it is never enough simply to be satisfied that they are held together in tension. We must work at integrating the two emphases — Christ as personal Savior and Christ as Lord over all creation, including all of the various spheres of cultural activity.

Our text points to one way of getting at this important task of integration. It does so by suggesting a way of thinking about Christ's relationship to the creation as an intimate one. Let me explain why intimacy is important to the integrative task. The very personal sense of belonging expressed in Heidelberg One is pervaded by a sense of intimacy: I can take comfort in the knowledge that I belong to Jesus, not only because I am in some general sense his property, but also because he gave himself in an intimate and deeply caring way for me, paying the debt of my sin with his own blood. And he promised me his presence: He will be with me to the end; he is a faithful Savior who will never forsake those who belong to him. Though I walk through the valley of the shadow of death I will fear no evil — not simply because I belong to him — but because *he is with me.*

As we move toward a focus on the more cosmic authority of Jesus Christ, however, there is a danger that we will lose this sense of intimacy. This in turn can promote a pattern wherein we think of our personal growth in Christ in terms of spiritual warmth, but our extensive growth in Christ comes to be characterized by an impersonal distancing. And Kuyper's manifesto about Christ's cosmic lordship does not quite give us enough to get beyond this problem. Jesus owns every square inch of the creation, Kuyper tells us. But we are led to think of this ownership as a dimension of his ascended rule over all things: Jesus stands "above" all that he owns, claiming his kingly right to obedience from us in every sphere of human interaction.

This is good as far as it goes. Indeed, it is for us Calvinists an inescapable follow-through of that sixteenth-century heritage that we are also celebrating on this Reformation Sunday. One historian of Protestantism has remarked that for Reformed Christians, the theme of the sixteenth century was "Only Christ *saves*," while the theme of the seventeenth century was "Only Christ *rules*." For those of us in the Kuyperian stream of Dutch Calvinism, however, the subsequent centuries were important times for working out the "ruling" theme for all of human culture. And this theme has served us well as a way of making a very basic point about the reign of Jesus Christ and its implication for liberal arts education. Our passage here in Ephesians reinforces the point: the One whose measure we are to grow into is the same One who ascended on high so that he might exercise his kingly rule. But the apostle quickly adds an important clarification: to say that he ascended cannot be understood apart from a recognition that "he had also descended into the lower parts of the earth . . . so that he might fill all things" (Eph. 4:9).

Let me put it simply: *Jesus went deep.* He descended into the deepest parts of creation, experiencing in an intimate way the full reality of its woundedness. An ancient teacher of the church, Gregory Nazianzus, put the matter nicely: "What he did not assume, he could not heal." Jesus could only apply his healing touch to that which he experienced by entering into the depths of our suffering and brokenness.

The story is told of Pope John XIII that when he was still an Italian cardinal he was having dinner one night with one of his priestly assistants. The young priest was reporting to the cardinal about another priest, a real renegade, who was doing things that were embarrassing to the hierarchy. The future pope listened calmly, sipping wine from a goblet. Finally the assistant cried out, "Why are you not upset and angry? Don't you realize what this priest is doing?" The cardinal then asked, "Father, whose goblet is this?" "It is yours, your grace," he answered. The cardinal then threw the goblet to the floor, and it shattered into many fragments. "And now whose goblet is it?" he asked. "It is still yours," was the answer. "And so is this priest still my brother in Christ," said the cardinal, "even though he is shattered and broken."

Jesus descended into the depths of a fragmented creation. He came into the world not to condemn it, but that the world through him might be saved. What he now rules over, he gave his life for. He assumed the cosmic brokenness that he came to heal. This has important lessons for Christian liberal arts learning and scholarship. We too must enter into the depths of that which we are called to study.

Craig Dykstra put it well in a speech he gave a few years ago to the Indiana Academy of Religion. Religious educational communities can serve us all well, he observed, by training people "who see deeply into the reality of things and who love that reality." That is an important way of stating the maturity mandate for Calvin College: We can get beyond merely embracing the tensions between piety and learning by fostering a piety *for* learning, by becoming the kind of people who see deeply into the reality of things and who love that reality — for the Savior who shed his blood for us also descended into the deep places of the creation so that he might fill all things. Jesus not only rules over every square inch of the creation, he also *loves* those square inches. And his love goes so deep that he still suffers in and over the brokenness of the cosmos. We cannot demonstrate his rule without also demonstrating his love for the cosmic reality that he came to save.

And so, members of the Calvin College community — Gaylen and Sue Byker, faculty, administration, staff, students, trustees, alumni, friends — here is a word from the Lord for you on this important occasion: *Go deep!* Jesus went deep into the distorted and fragmented creation, taking on all that he wanted to heal. He descended into the lower parts so that he might fill all things.

As we attempt to promote Christian maturity in higher education, we must never lose the very personal dimension of this mandate. Thomas Schmidt, in discussing the spiritual resources for Christian patience in his recent book on sexuality, tells a moving story about Mabel, a woman to whom he paid some pastoral visits. Mabel suffered from cancer for at least two decades. Her body was constantly invaded by tumors, and when Schmidt got to know her she was blind and a permanent resident of a health care facility. On one of his visits he found her, as usual, sitting quietly near her bed. The air around her was permeated with the smells and sounds of dying humanity. He asked her, "Mabel, how do you spend your time in these surroundings?" She immediately responded that she constantly talked to Jesus, and then she began to sing in a voice that was weak but full of confidence: "Jesus is all the world to me, My life, my joy, my all. He is my strength from day to day; Without him I would fall."

Jesus fills all things — he is all the world to us. And that is a matter of great comfort to us as individuals. But Jesus must also be all the world to us in our dedication to the cause of liberal arts education. We must not only study the fossil record, we must look deeply into it and love it. We must not only study family life, we must look deeply into it and love it. We must not only love the record of human achievement and failure, but we must also look deeply into it and love it. We must not only study the human psyche in all of its complex brokenness, we must look deeply into that psyche and love it. The earth is the Lord's — in all of its confusion and brokenness — and the fullness thereof, the world and all who dwell therein. Jesus entered into the deep places so that he might fill all things.

Go deep, Gaylen Byker. Go deep, Calvin College. Liberal arts institutions desperately need this kind of worldview depth. They need people who love the reality that they are studying and who go deep in their relationship with that reality. Higher education is afflicted these days by a pervasive sense of fragmentation and disconnectedness. It is important that we propose an alternative.

In Plato's dialogue *Meno*, Socrates' friends have been trying under his prodding to arrive at a unified definition of virtue. They keep coming up with different examples and definitions and they get very discouraged. Finally they say to Socrates in their frustration: "Look, all we've come up with is a swarm of definitions and examples and we don't seem to get beyond the swarm." Socrates responds by telling them not to be discouraged by swarms. In spite of the appearances, he says, "all nature is akin"; and this means that there is nothing to hinder us, having tackled just one small thing in our quest for a unified knowledge, from going on to find out about all the rest, just as long as we do not grow weary in the seeking.

As Christians we can agree with Socrates when he insists that "all nature is akin." But we can take our confidence from a very different source. We know that the earth is the Lord's in all of its fullness. And we also know that after that world had become broken and fragmented by sin, Jesus Christ entered into the deep places, in order to fill all things — and that now all things hold together in him. It is because he "is all the world" to us that we can lovingly study his world.

Go deep, Calvin College. Go deep, so that we may all "come to the unity of the faith and of the knowledge of the Son of God, to maturity, to the full stature of Christ." Amen.

Dream of the School

Lionel Basney

Late, in the dead space of the night
after midnight, I heard a door click
shut behind me. I stood in the groove of a room,

its walls tight against my shoulders.
On the walls, shelves; on the shelves, books.
They stretched as far as I could see.

Then, two others. From the first I caught
the sickle cut of sweat. The other seemed,
in that gloom, to stand in a glimmer of starch.

"Wat moet jij hier? Do you know where you are?"
His voice seemed hoarse, as from the dust of ploughing.
"Nosce te ipsum," I said. "I know where I am."

"Then why these tears?" "I've sold my life for books,"
I said. "There are too many of them,
too little wisdom for the time I've spent."

Then the other, *oma,* took my elbow
and shook me. "We gave our money
to build this place," she said. *"Kom aan."*

Then on the wall of books I seemed
to see all those our burning cities
have sent to trudge the highways, age on age,

saw Cordelia heal the ruined king.
"Do you know what you are doing," said my guide,
"when you tell our stories? You are making

the wordless dead live out their fears again
within the long permission of God's hope."
Then on the wall, the brand of an exact number,

and an image folding to a pattern
unimaginable except by number,
like a galaxy hinging on nothing.

"Do you know what you are doing?
You reach for the stop of time itself
inside the envelope of God's intentions."

"But to what end?" I said. I felt fear, as before.
But she reached and shook me, as before.
"You cannot know," she said, "what your words

will weigh with students remembering them
in a place you will never see.
You work in the bewilderment of time.

The harrow kicks the stone away
and in a hundred years the hill is changed.
Therefore have faith, hope to do good,

love the work and its woven pattern:
read, talk, listen, cook, lay brick, sweep
the mat when it is drenched with snow,

wash the beaker, run the errand, pray
for the healing of what you cannot heal."
Then the walls in the night fell away

and I was alone. My eyes met wind,
and the dawn in fog, buildings in trees,
and on the bright plain of the campus,

people walking, from dark to light to dark
to light, under the trees, in the open.

The Embarrassment of Riches

Gaylen J. Byker

As I gaze around me at this welcome crowd of witnesses, members of the Board of Trustees, faculty and administrative colleagues, distinguished guests, alumni and students, friends and family, and as I think about this occasion — which I scarcely would have considered possible a year ago — I feel a sense of joy and excitement as together we embark upon a new administration, a new stage, in the life of Calvin College. When I proposed the theme of these inaugural activities — "Keeping Faith: Embracing the Tensions in Christian Higher Education" — there were numerous objections to the use of the word "tensions" in the context of a celebration. But, in keeping with Dr. Mouw's message last evening on the "Maturity Mandate," I prefer to use these events, and the opportunity for reflection they offer, to do something more than mark an important transition in the history of Calvin College.

I want to challenge the Calvin community to build and maintain the intellectual, emotional, and spiritual courage required to keep faith with the best elements of Calvin's distinctive history. I believe that this will require a willingness to embrace the tensions in Christian higher education, to take risks, and to make sacrifices. We must heed the words Henry Stob said a generation ago; a "mind of safety" will not be adequate for a mature Calvin College.

The challenge I want to propose grows out of my personal philosophy of life, my operational worldview. This philosophy, this worldview, has come into clearer focus over the past decade, in large

11

part because of my experiences in the Middle East and my encounters with the parables of Jesus seen from the perspective of the Middle Eastern peasants who first heard them. Out of these experiences and encounters have emerged a "theology of risk-taking" and a mode of living that I believe can be useful for understanding and dealing with the tensions inherent in the current stage of Calvin's history. My theology of risk-taking also helps to explain why I agreed to accept the presidency of the college.

My theology is rooted in the life of Jesus and the message of his parables. Jesus apparently began his training as a rabbi at the customary age of twelve and mastered the Jewish scriptures and traditions. And, contrary to the common perception that he was a teller of simple stories, he was, in fact, an amazingly sophisticated metaphorical theologian — in complete command of the idiom of first-century oral tradition. He was recognized as an authoritative teacher in his first reported public discourses. His lessons were couched in the metaphors and images used in the theological debates of his day, but he used them to shock and challenge the religious establishment. And, as important as the contents of Jesus' parables are, their form and structure may be even more important for conveying the essence of his message about the kingdom of God. Time after time he compared the kingdom of God to a character in a story. These stories were not ordinary, predictable morality tales — but stories with twists and turns that his audience must have found bizarre. They were based on unorthodox premises, they violated polite manners and important social mores. They had surprise endings, or in some cases, like the parable of the Father and the Two Lost Sons, the endings were missing entirely, leaving it to the hearers to supply their own responses to the open issues.

James Breech, noted scholar of biblical narrative, maintained that the pattern of the parables, the meaning conveyed by their structure, is the essence of Jesus' message. He was saying, in effect, that citizens of the kingdom of God are people who live like the characters in his stories. That is, they willingly live with the bizarre twists and turns of life, the surprising or unknown endings. They are free to call into question the conventions of the world around them and reject the norms and practices of Pharisaic society. This liberated way of living allows those of us who follow Jesus, in fact entices us, to take risks for the kingdom, to sacrifice our need for certainty and security.[1] I try to live this way. In fact, that is why I was open to the call to become president of Calvin College, even though I wasn't looking for a new job, and this job didn't fit my immediate plans. Yet, here we are today. And, upon reflection, I am struck by the number of Calvin alumni and faculty I have met in key places in this country and around the world who are doing exciting work in God's kingdom because they also try to live this way.

So, why should I and other Calvin alumni and faculty attempt to live as if in parables, accepting the tensions of uncertainty and unknown endings? I believe that the courage to live this way is drawn from the reality captured in the radical, existentialist opening question and answer of the sixteenth-century Heidelberg Catechism. The question asks, "What is your *only* comfort in life and in death?" The radical word here is "only." The question is not, "What is your *primary* comfort" or "What is your *most important* comfort" or "What is your comfort of *last resort?*" It asks, "What is your *only* comfort," the only one you need, the only real comfort there is. And you know the answer, perhaps even by heart: "My only comfort is that I am not my own — but belong, body and soul, in life and in death — to my faithful Savior Jesus Christ." This seemingly modern question, with its historic Christian response, recognizes that we have and need only one firm reference point. And with that one firm reference point we are free to live as real-life characters in Jesus' parables.

Which brings us back to the inaugural theme: keeping faith by embracing the tensions in Christian higher education. I believe that keeping faith with the best of Calvin's history means always reforming and always improving the education, the scholarship, the art, and the service of the college. It means being prepared to adapt to the rapidly changing world in which we live and work and in which our students must function in the twenty-first century. To keep faith with Calvin's history, to live up to the promise of Calvin's childhood and adolescence, we must have intellectual, emotional, and spiritual courage, the willingness to take risks and make sacri-

1. James Breech, *The Silence of Jesus: The Authentic Voice of the Historical Man* (Philadelphia: Fortress Press, 1983).

fices. We not only must deal with the tensions, we must *embrace* them.

Embrace is an action one does not ordinarily associate with tensions. The very word *tension* makes many people, well, tense. It tightens muscles. It produces emotional stress. We usually think of avoiding, eliminating, or resolving tensions to relieve our anxieties about them and the need to expend mental energy on them. And Christians do struggle with the tensions caused by brokenness and sin in our lives and in our world.

However, many tensions are beneficial, even necessary; tensions that are built into creation itself. There is the finely tuned tension of a violin string that makes beautiful music possible. Or the "antagonistic muscles" that operate in tension in our bodies so that we can stand up, walk about, or move our arms. Or the carefully designed tensions that hold this building together. The Constitution of the United States was crafted with the tension of checks and balances. St. Augustine grappled creatively with tensions inherent in the gospel — God's love and God's judgment — and living simultaneously as a citizen of this world and as a citizen of the kingdom of God. John Calvin wrestled fruitfully with the tension between free will and human responsibility on the one hand and divine sovereignty and providence on the other. Calvinists, it has long been said, pray as if everything depends on God and work as if everything depends on them. Abraham Kuyper struggled productively with the tension between common grace and the antithesis.

We, individually and as a community, have learned to cope with a variety of tensions; at times we do a good job of balancing them. I want to lay down the challenge today, however, that we go even further and deeper, to build and maintain the intellectual, emotional, and spiritual courage to embrace the tensions in Christian higher education generally and at Calvin College in particular. The challenge is that we must capitalize on the strengths, creativity, and motivations for thought and action inherent in the interplay among these tensions. We should be "maximalists," seeking the benefits of the interplay or even integration, while avoiding the snares at the polar extremes.

Those of us who are inheritors of the culture and Reformed tradition that was transplanted to North America from the Netherlands are well accustomed to the tensions of which I will speak today. I take my title for this address, "The Embarrassment of Riches," from a masterwork of the same name by Harvard historian Simon Schama. In *The Embarrassment of Riches* Schama illustrates in great detail how tension fostered the rise of the Dutch Golden Age of the seventeenth century. He describes how this small Calvinistic country became the wealthiest on earth and the "arbiter of the world" by embracing the unresolved dilemma, the enduring tension, between being wealthy and being moral. He concludes that it was the wrestling with the dilemma, the embracing, if you will, of this tension that produced an era of flourishing art and education, republican government, tolerance, and public works projects of unprecedented scale.

Schama identifies what he terms "the moral geography of the Dutch mind" in this tension-packed passage:

> [It was] adrift between the fear of the deluge and the hope of moral salvage, in the tidal ebb and flow between worldliness and homeliness, between the gratification of appetite and its denial, between the conditional consecration of wealth and perdition in its surfeit. . . . To be Dutch . . . was to live in a perpetual present participle, to cohabit with the unsettled. . . . To be Dutch still means coming to terms with the moral ambiguities of materialism in their own idiosyncratic but inescapable ways: through the daily living of it, in Sunday sermons on nuclear weapons and Monday rites of scrubbing the sidewalk.[2]

On the eve of the twenty-first century, there are an array of such tensions that confront all higher education that aims to be Christian, and some that confront us in particular ways at Calvin. I want to highlight the most pressing of these tensions to outline the task ahead if we are to keep faith by embracing them.

1. *The tension between piety and intellect.* There is a fragile balance that can easily be lost between efforts to develop and maintain piety

2. Simon Schama, *The Embarrassment of Riches: An Interpretation of Dutch Culture in the Golden Age* (Berkeley: University of California Press, 1988), p. 609.

and efforts to develop the mind and the intellect through education in the liberal arts. Those more concerned with a character of piety worry about a focus on the life of the mind and where it might take the college. Those who stress the need for intellectual development decry anti-intellectualism and fear that a shallow, personally focused emphasis on pietistic feelings and practices will limit the intellectual development of students and faculty. But Calvinism, at its best, is at the crossroads of searching inquiry and spiritual devotion. The challenge is to keep this creative debate alive and, in the words of Yale University historian Harry Stout, a Calvin alumnus, to make "intellect and piety mutually reinforcing instead of mutually antagonistic."[3]

2. *The tension between teaching and scholarship.* The education of Calvin's students and the scholarly pursuits of its faculty can be enriched through a fruitful embrace of the tension between teaching and scholarship that continually looks for ways to leverage one for the benefit of the other.

3. *The tension between the needs and desires of individuals and the needs of the community.* For faculty, professionalization and disciplinary specialization compete for time and attention with interdisciplinary undertakings, participation in campuswide dialogue and events, and interaction with students outside of class. For students, job orientation and preoccupation with self can come at the expense of liberal arts breadth and involvement in community activities and in the lives of others.

4. *The tension between living in a science-based, technology-driven modern society and carrying out the college's mission to teach that there are eternal truths and transcendent values.* The courageous embrace of the tension between technology-driven modernity and a Christian liberal arts education places us at the cutting edge of technology and media. We must be there to serve as informed and responsible participants in the debate about technology's uses — and limits. We

3. Harry Stout, "The Ghosts of Puritan Die Hard: Interview with Harry Stout. By Kyle Farley," *Dialogue* (Jan./Feb. 1995): 32-36.

need to have the confidence displayed by our Communication Arts and Sciences and Computer departments to be skilled agents of cultural impact and change, as our response to the unchanging gospel of Jesus Christ.

5. *The tension between motivating students and faculty through public recognition of achievement or promise of material rewards and the Calvin community's preference for an egalitarian community environment, modesty, and inner motivation.* The embrace of this tension will help us to avoid the potential excesses at either pole, while keeping alive the debate about the proper balance between external and internal motivations for personal best efforts.

6. *The tension between wealth and its obligations.* Material riches are frequently seen here at Calvin — as they were by the Dutch of the seventeenth century — to be in tension with morality and stewardship. The tension is amplified in the seemingly contradictory texts in the Bible affirming material prosperity — even abundance — as God's blessing and those condemning riches as a curse. The dangers of materialism and its excesses are tugging against the privilege of enjoying the fruits of God's creation and the need for significant resources to carry out our mission with adequate facilities and budgets. Professor John Schneider of our faculty has served us well by thoughtfully analyzing the tension between the possession and enjoyment of material wealth and the requirements of Christian stewardship, morality, and charity. His book *Godly Materialism: Rethinking Money and Possessions*[4] is a first-rate example of how we as Reformed Christians at Calvin College can creatively embrace the tensions that confront us.

7. *The tension between a college or university's adherence to a distinctive Christian tradition and the drive for academic excellence and academic freedom.* This tension has existed throughout the history of higher education in America. In his widely read book *The Soul of the American University,* George Marsden describes how several hundred

---

4. John Schneider, *Godly Materialism: Rethinking Money and Possessions* (Downers Grove: InterVarsity Press, 1994).

American colleges and universities — from Harvard and Yale to the University of Michigan and Vanderbilt — resolved this tension. Through a series of gradual changes, most often in the name of academic excellence and academic freedom, they became thoroughly secular institutions. Few Christian academic institutions have maintained their religious character for more than 150 years.[5] Again, I believe that we must boldly embrace this tension. We must defy the precedent. We must beat the odds. We must be distinctively Reformed Christians *and* academically excellent. We must be academically excellent *because* we are Reformed Christians. We must remain a prime, attractive example of why there should always be what Marsden calls "institutional pluralism" — that is, a variety among institutions — rather than succumbing to the impulse that all colleges and universities become uniform and devoid of distinctive religious features.

8. *The tension between Calvin's distinctive cultural identity and the need for diversity within the faculty and student body.* The scope and claims of the Christian faith are far broader than any college or denomination. Diversity is an important component of an excellent liberal arts education. Calvin's cultural heritage includes features that are valuable and important to maintain, a dedication to family and liberal education, a loyalty to the work ethic even while calling into question popular American mores and materialism. Calvin's cultural heritage also has baggage that must be abandoned — unequal treatment of women, tendencies toward isolation, a "chosen people" complex, and lack of hospitality toward those who are ethnically or culturally different. When we embrace the tension between our cultural identity and need for diversity we will evaluate carefully the components of Calvin's culture, to see what is valuable and what is harmful. We will emerge from this exercise a community that is more diverse and more welcoming — a better reflection of God's kingdom.

So, on this morning of inauguration, at the dawn of a new administration, I pose these questions: Can we live confidently and

---

5. George Marsden, *The Soul of the American University: From Protestant Establishment to Established Non-Belief* (New York: Oxford University Press, 1994).

creatively as characters in parables with unknown endings? Will we remember that we have only *one* comfort in life and in death? Can we muster the intellectual, emotional, and spiritual courage to face head-on the difficult issues and decisions that confront us? Will we embrace the tensions? For as the embarrassment of riches fostered a golden age in the seventeenth century, our embrace of the tensions facing Calvin College can be our way of living up to our potential, our maturity mandate.

Former Calvin President William Spoelhof — my president — tells a story that beautifully illustrates what I have been talking about. He begins by recalling his childhood years in New Jersey, growing up in a home with blue Delft tiles hanging on the walls, bearing proverbs. On one of them is painted, "Van het concert des levens krijgt niemand een program." In English it means "For the concert of life no one gets a program." This is Dr. Spoelhof's favorite proverb, but he wisely calls it a "half-good" proverb. For in the concert of life, although there may be no program, there is a Conductor. Dr. Spoelhof understands very well the underlying tension of this proverb. God is the Conductor, and every now and then God allows us to hear, and even play, some grace notes.

This ceremony is a formal acknowledgment of a transition, the beginning of a new chapter in the life of Calvin College. I wish to begin not with the end in mind, but with agreement on the quality and character that our lives and actions should have. I trust, God helping us, that it will be said of this administration that we acted boldly to safeguard what is distinctive and most valuable about this college. I trust, and expect, that our legacy will be one of embracing the tensions, of having the intellectual, emotional, and spiritual courage to face head-on the difficult issues and decisions that confront us.

I invite you to keep company with me as we step out into the challenges and opportunities before us. I pray that we will follow the example of Dr. Spoelhof and all those who understand the message and meaning of the blue Delft proverb. I pray that we will keep our eyes on the Conductor each step of the way.

Piety and Progress:
A History of Calvin College

James D. Bratt and Ronald A. Wells

On 18 February 1876 the Reverend Gerrit E. Boer formally opened the institution from which Calvin College would be born, the theological school of the True Dutch Reformed Church at Grand Rapids, Michigan. The occasion presented Boer with ample challenges. His class of seven students featured varying ages and levels of academic preparation. He faced competition and distraction from noises within and without: from within, because his classroom occupied the second floor (the "upper room," it was soon called) above the parochial grade school sponsored by Boer's 1,300-member congregation; from without, because the building stood hard by Grand Rapids's main railroad yards, lending his instruction the accompaniment of switch engines rumbling, shrieking, and clanging about. But Boer's most daunting challenge doubtless lay in the seventeen-subject curriculum he had to teach all by himself. The list included typical seminary subjects — isogogics and exegetics, dogmatics and hermeneutics — but also a compressed combination of high school and college courses, the most notable of which were the languages that his farm boys and shop hands were expected to master: German, Latin, Greek, and Hebrew.[1]

1. John J. Timmerman, *Promises to Keep: A Centennial History of Calvin*

This essay will appear in similar form in Richard T. Hughes and William B. Adrian, eds., *Models for Christian Higher Education: Strategies for Survival and Success in the Twenty-first Century* (Grand Rapids: Eerdmans, 1997).

Nearly a quarter century would pass before Calvin College emerged as an institution in its own right, and twenty years more before it would be granting baccalaureate degrees. The seminary spun off a college preparatory "Literary Department" in 1900; this developed into a two-year junior college by 1906 and a full, four-year college in 1920. But most of the salient features of the college's history were present in that upper room in 1876.

The college, first and foremost, belonged to a church, whose name — True, Dutch, and Reformed — testified to its sectarian tenacity, its ethnic identity, and its comprehensive theology. The denomination was born in 1857 among recent Dutch immigrants to western Michigan as a breakaway from the Reformed Church in America (RCA), an institution dating back to colonial New Netherlands. The split was legitimated on grounds of orthodoxy, as a "return to the standpoint of the fathers." This standpoint had been reasserted, and in these same words, already back in the Netherlands in the 1834 "Secession" *(Afscheiding)* of dozens of congregations from that country's established church. Since Seceders were present not only among the True Reformed but equally among the RCA loyalists in 1857, Calvin College's forebears might be said to qualify as sectarians twice over, a remnant within a remnant, a posture not usually associated with broad and generous liberal arts education.[2]

That form has often held true. Calvin's professors from Boer's time onward have had to deal with suspicions, complaints, and charges of heresy on issues ranging from the fundamental to the trivial. More difficult still for an *academic* institution, the complaints

---

College (Grand Rapids: Eerdmans, 1975), pp. 13-18. Timmerman's is the most accessible of the college's histories, but we rely as well on Henry J. Ryskamp, "The History of Calvin College and Seminary" (unpublished MS in Calvin College and Seminary archives [1967]), upon which Timmerman often depended and which contains much additional information. Another valuable study is George Stob, "The Christian Reformed Church and Her Schools" (unpublished Th.D. dissertation, Princeton Theological Seminary, 1955), chaps. 8-13.

2. For the denomination's history, see James D. Bratt, *Dutch Calvinism in Modern America: A History of a Conservative Subculture* (Grand Rapids: Eerdmans, 1984), pp. 3-13, 37-40; and more thoroughly, Diedrich H. Kromminga, *The Christian Reformed Tradition: From the Reformation to the Present* (Grand Rapids: Eerdmans, 1943).

have involved behavior as well as ideas, or behavior as sure token of ideas, with faculty and students being held to strict tests on both. In the earliest instances Boer was called to account for speaking at the funeral of an RCA minister, while the school's first professor with a doctorate, Geerhardus Vos, was harassed for teaching the minority, supralapsarian position on divine election.[3] In years ahead the regulation of student conduct particularly with respect to movie attendance would be the greatest burden the faculty felt, and their greatest shortcoming in the eyes of ecclesiastical monitors. In short, the sectarian tradition placed tight constraints on educational maneuvering. For disruptive "noises within," Boer's heirs might have preferred the commotion of schoolchildren.

If the True (after 1890, "Christian") Reformed had the soul of a sect, however, they had the memory of a national church. The "standpoint" that they upheld was that of the Synod of Dort, an international gathering of no mean talent, and Dort meant not only five-point Calvinism but a polity that made the church custodian and critic of national culture. To fulfill this role pastors needed to be educated in the liberal arts; to faithfully exegete Scripture and propound Reformed theology, they had to know the biblical and scholarly languages. Hence Rev. Boer's comprehensive and language-heavy curriculum. Christian Reformed laity before 1900 might not have been well educated themselves but they insisted that their pastors be. Orthodoxy demanded it.

Their cultural mandate gained great vigor under the Neo-Calvinist movement that arose in the Netherlands after 1870 under the leadership of Abraham Kuyper.[4] Kuyper's career was inspiration enough for the most ambitious youth: conversant in many disciplines, a writer of infinite capacities, an institution-founder par excellence, he served successively as pastor, politician, professor, and eventually prime minister of the Netherlands. More inspiring still was the mission he gave his followers, to renew Dutch society and culture by dint of their Calvinistic critique and constructions. Indeed, Kuyper opened the whole world for Christian participation;

3. Stob, "CRC Schools," pp. 191-93, 213-17.
4. For the most convenient English-language overview of Kuyper, see Bratt, *Dutch Calvinism,* pp. 14-33, and the annotated bibliography, pp. 313-14.

as his most famous dictum put it: "There is not a square inch on the whole plain of human existence over which Christ, who is Lord over all, does not proclaim: 'This is Mine!' "[5] Notably, this statement came in an address (1880) opening the Neo-Calvinists' new Free University, which Kuyper founded to develop leadership for his movement and which he placed in Amsterdam, the nation's capital.

"Kuyperianism," then, meant broad and fresh cultural engagement — windows open to the world. But it also meant persistent argument, sometimes a shouting match, through those windows. Kuyper wanted to take on the reigning mentalities of modern culture at the level of fundamental principle. He demanded that Christians build a comprehensive worldview and pit it in full battle against those of secularism, humanism, and naturalism. Appropriately for a modern anti-modernist, Kuyper left a double legacy. Some of his followers, the "positive" Calvinists, listened most to his lessons on "common grace," the heritage of divine blessing that allowed people of all faiths and none to achieve moral and intellectual good. On that basis Christians were to seek out and harvest all the world's treasures, redeeming them to the glory of God. But others harkened more to Kuyper's insistence that an "antithesis" lay between the fundamental commitments of the regenerate and the worldly, that Christians ought therefore to go their own way in all things and stay critical of opposing systems.[6] Bringing together all these camps, the two sorts of Neo-Calvinists as well as the pietist Seceders, thus added to the noise within Calvin College but also endowed it with a truly creative tension. The tensions were kept in harness by the "noise without," by the clamoring engines of modernity that Boer heard literally and his descendants figuratively. Some at Calvin would try to sort these out, others to drown them out; a few hoped to take the throttle. But no one could ignore the traffic. The world without fixed the college within.

All this noise should not obscure some of the plainer virtues in

---

5. Abraham Kuyper, "Souvereiniteit in Eigen Kring" (Amsterdam: Kruyt, 1880), p. 32.

6. Bratt, *Dutch Calvinism*, pp. 18-20, 50-54; Henry Zwaanstra, *Reformed Thought and Experience in a New World: A Study of the Christian Reformed Church and Its American Environment, 1890-1918* (Kampen: Kok, 1973), pp. 95-131.

the upper room that proved essential to the college's character. First of all, the enterprise had exacted enormous labor from all involved, especially from the faculty. Rev. Boer not only had to teach his seventeen subjects but pastor a huge congregation and edit the denomination's magazine. The students caught their share of the load, too; the one item besides its solid curriculum and Christian stance that has regularly won notice from outside observers has been the work ethic, the seriousness of Calvin's students. Second, almost any student who has felt the call to take on these labors has been permitted to try. Calvin's admissions policy has been as anti-elitist as its curricular standards have been rigorous. These traits together bespeak an egalitarian culture, the fairer fruit of the sectarian tree. From the start and well past World War II, Calvin was known among the Christian Reformed as "our school"; it was the product and pride of a community. Every plausible candidate from that community was entitled to attend but then held to tough measure. Every faculty member was susceptible to a draft for additional, extramural labors. Every member of the denomination was taxed (by the denomination's quota system) the same amount to support the college, and every college-aged person was expected to give Calvin serious — in many cases, sole — consideration. Calvin's history cannot be understood apart from the benefits and constraints that come with a communal sociology; nor can its philosophical hallmark, Christian worldview construction and teaching within those parameters, be understood apart from the cycle of reinforcement it gave and received from communal solidarity.

*　　*　　*

The history of the college proper divides into four eras, each of which recast, yet also recycled, these themes. Between 1894 and 1920 the school slowly emerged from the shadow of the seminary with glimpses of bright promise for the future. From 1920 to 1945 that promise was tested by the cultural upheaval, economic depression, and wartime constraints of the outside world. Between 1945 and 1970 the college passed through two enormous expansions, a campus relocation, and a curricular overhaul, but all within its traditional parameters of vision and constituency. Since 1970 the communal walls have become notably more porous. Calvin's vision has attracted considerable outside attention, while its own house and supporting community now register far more external influences than ever before.

The movement toward a separate college began in 1894 when the CRC Synod first authorized the admission of other than pre-seminarians into the preparatory program.[7] But such students started to enroll in number only after 1900 when new curricular paths ("Classical" and "Scientific") were installed along with the faculty to teach them. Three of these faculty would define the college for years to come. Albertus Rooks served as principal of the literary department and as dean of the college from his appointment in 1894 until his retirement in 1941. He knew his constituency well and offered the calm practicality necessary to win their trust. Jacob G. Vanden Bosch presided over the English department from 1900 to 1945 from a pedestal of Victorian values that made literature safe for the college. But it was Barend Klaas Kuiper, the college's first history professor, who gave the most public direction.

Kuiper began his turbulent career on a high note in 1903 by writing a booklet to mobilize CRC support for a college of its own.[8] His tract sounded all the Kuyperian themes. He had grand visions of institution building. He insisted that no existing school (including, by name and at length, the RCA's Hope College) taught that thoroughgoing Calvinism which alone was adequate to stem the cultural tides of unbelief. But he then added another note, congruent with Vanden Bosch's gentility and long to endure even, perhaps especially, in the "progressive" circle on campus. He insisted that the CRC needed a college also to rescue "our people" from the materialism they had learned all too well from their immigrant struggles and from the models of success that America offered. The physical was a necessary but lower realm, Kuiper in-

7. This era is covered in Timmerman, *Promises,* chap. 2; Stob, "CRC Schools," chap. 10; Ryskamp, "History," chaps. 4-9; and by a principal architect-observer, Albertus J. Rooks, in "A History of Calvin College 1894-1926," *Semi-Centennial Volume: Theological School and Calvin College, 1876-1926* (Grand Rapids: Semi-Centennial Committee, 1926), pp. 49-90.

8. B[arend K.] Kuiper, *The Proposed Calvinistic College at Grand Rapids* (Grand Rapids: Sevensma, 1903).

toned; the spiritual was higher and led on to better ends, that is, a cultivation of "culture" in its own right, and the development of that wisdom which the church and nation so desperately needed. Calvin graduates should enter America to save the nation from its worst instincts; perhaps they might enter its more polished precincts at greater ease.

The voice of Seceder piety did not agree. Jacob Vanden Bosch noted that the college grew precisely with the CRC's Christian day-school movement, the former providing teachers for the latter and the two together rising along with Dutch-American social standing on the one hand and the secularization of the public schools on the other. Prosperity and impiety, perversely, would be the making of the college — but only if kept "out there." The need for a safe place to send their children was the one consistent note in all apologias for the fledgling school. Such a sanctuary would save "our youth" for the faith, train leaders for the church, and allow the group to glean just the untainted fruit from the American horn of plenty.[9]

These two visions clashed at the dawn of Calvin's next era. The immediate source of the conflict lay in World War I, a cause that the positive Calvinists had championed but which turned into a trauma of forced acculturation for the CRC.[10] Now the set-upon took revenge, ousting the leading progressive from the Calvin Seminary faculty and giving the college's new president, the Reverend J. J. Hiemenga, a cold shower of suspicion. Barely had the first graduating class of the full four-year college marched across the stage in 1921 than the complaint was sounded across the denomination. Had Calvin lost its distinctiveness? Was it not emphasizing physical plant over principle, pursuing worldly eminence instead of simple faithfulness? The plaintiffs' evidence ran from the Glee Club's programming Catholic songs to the pride everyone took in the sparkling new (1917) campus. The watchdogs also sniffed at the

9. Jacob Vanden Bosch, "The School and Christian Education," in *Semi-Centennial Volume*, pp. 147-48. See also Louis Berkhof, "Our School's Reason for Existence and the Preservation Thereof," ibid., pp. 127-29.

10. The war and its aftermath are covered in Bratt, *Dutch Calvinism*, pp. 83-104. On the controversy discussed in this paragraph, see Stob, "CRC Schools," pp. 351-70, and Timmerman, *Promises*, pp. 46-52.

words of Hiemenga himself. The president wanted Calvin to rate as "one of the most efficient . . . complete . . . [and] thorough" colleges in the land, "able to compete with any institution of its kind. . . . [Its] policy must be to compete and surpass, not to knock and criticize."[11] Hiemenga added that the school should maintain its "uniqueness" by standing on "the principles of Calvinism," but his hearers thought his heart lay more with the former than with the latter sentiments. He brought to office a go-getter spirit that irked the faculty, and launched a campaign for a $1 million endowment that left the constituency cold. When only $90,000 of new money came in, Hiemenga went back to the pastorate in 1925.

The Christian Reformed were not being tight, only scared. Having been force-marched into American life, they were determined to maintain some sort of distance from the world. They accomplished this through the Synodical excision of three forms of heresy in the early 1920s and through the Synodical prohibition of three forms of worldly amusements in 1928.[12] In other words Calvin College had the ill fate — or Providence — to be launched simultaneously with the 1920s' moral revolution. Well past that decade its students would be closely monitored for signs of "flaming youth." The faculty were drafted to be enforcers, and the movies (one of the fatalities of 1928) were made the moral boundary. No issue provoked more student dissent, constituent worry, or faculty fatigue from 1920 to 1965 than the prohibition on movie attendance. And no one paid a higher price than B. K. Kuiper, who lost his faculty position in 1928 for apologizing with too many words and too little contrition for having gone to shows.[13]

Under pietist winds the college hugged the shore. Its students were taught solid skills, basic science, and the Western classics under the careful guidance of teachers. Their time outside of class divided between working for room and board and participating in the myriad clubs that functioned like nineteenth-century college liter-

11. Quotations from John J. Hiemenga, "Our Own Calvin," *Calvin Annual, 1920* (Grand Rapids: Calvin College, 1920), p. 30. Hiemenga's larger statement of purpose appears in "A Proposed Educational Program," *The Banner* 54 (November 13, 1919): 711.

12. Bratt, *Dutch Calvinism*, pp. 93-119.

13. Stob, "CRC Schools," pp. 370-81; Timmerman, *Promises*, pp. 37-38.

ary societies — enhancing student initiative, intensive research, public rhetoric, and cultural breadth. Little time went into intercollegiate athletics. The faculty grudgingly permitted a basketball team in 1920 but drew the line at football and fraternities. Calvin would never have either. The graduates of this era went out into the world — or more often, back into the denominational loop — as decent professionals and respectable citizens, stronger on ethical probity than on stirring vision.[14]

Curricularly, Calvin's main additions in this era occurred in the natural sciences. Yet the three key faculty appointments came elsewhere and provided whatever boldness of leadership the college had. Henry J. Ryskamp joined the faculty in 1918 as its first bona fide social scientist; he replaced Rooks as dean in 1941 and proved his prowess by flourishing despite a reputation for liberal politics. Seymour Swets, founder of the music program in 1923, won Calvin more respect from more people than did anyone else through his public direction of high classical repertoire. But the most momentous appointment was that of William Harry Jellema in 1921. The philosophy department that he founded won Calvin a national academic reputation and produced its first figures of international renown. Jellema himself introduced hundreds of students from other disciplines to the exhilaration of good Socratic method, to the possibility that truth was not a catechism to be memorized but a challenge to be sought out and humbly served.[15]

If this was stimulating to students, it was worrisome to critics. As professor of classics, Ralph Stob had found Jellema's Christianity too close to Greek Idealism; made president (1933), he encouraged Jellema's departure for Indiana University in 1936. But Stob's repeti-

---

14. Ryskamp, "History," pp. 116-32; Timmerman, *Promises,* pp. 61-66, 76.
15. Bratt, *Dutch Calvinism,* pp. 150-51; Timmerman, *Promises,* pp. 64, 81-82; Ryskamp, "History," pp. 142-43, 176-78, 327-28. Some indication of Jellema's impact in particular and the college's in general is evident in the reflections of Alvin Plantinga and Nicholas Wolterstorff in Kelly J. Clark, ed., *Philosophers Who Believe: The Spiritual Journey of Eleven Leading Thinkers* (Downers Grove: InterVarsity Press, 1993), pp. 50-59, 268-71. Notably, Frederick Manfred, one of the "renegade" novelists Calvin produced in this era, dedicated his barely fictionalized memoir of the place to Jellema (Feike Feikema, *The Primitive* [Garden City, N.Y.: Doubleday, 1949]).

tion of the rhetoric of distinctive Calvinism did not assure the pious that its substance was in place. Stob went back to Greek in 1939, leaving the way open for an extraordinary Board of Trustees inquisition into faculty instruction and student behavior. The former yielded up their syllabi for examination, the latter signed pledge cards promising conformity, the board deliberated to its satisfaction.[16] Then all parties joined to watch the world descend into war.

*   *   *

World War II knocked Calvin's enrollment back almost 20 percent, from 520 in 1941 to 420 in 1944. The slump triggered memories of the Depression-era trough (340 in 1933), but the reality never got that bad. Rather, Calvin soared with the postwar education boom into a new epoch in its history. Enrollment tripled in two years, from 420 in 1944 to 1,245 in 1946, and rose steadily thereafter to peak at 3,575 in 1968.[17] This expansion bespoke some fundamental changes but also hid some remarkable continuities and required a combination of daring and sense of tradition that was personified by William Spoelhof. His presidency (1951-1976) more than any other shaped the character and destiny of the college.

Most notable among the continuities would be the ethno-religious composition of the student body: 90 percent would still be coming from Christian Reformed congregations in 1970, at which date the CRC remained heavily Dutch in ethnic background and permitted but modest latitude in doctrine and liturgy. As for the faculty, all two hundred of them would still belong to the CRC and send their children to Christian schools as custom and contract required. On the side of change, the most obvious were a new campus and a new curriculum, but the more momentous probably lay in new expectations on either side of the podium. College education became less an entree into than a privilege of middle-class status for Calvin students in this period, while the Ph.D. changed from being a distant goal to being a terminal expectation on the

16. Ryskamp, "History," pp. 158-59, 174-88; Stob, "CRC Schools," pp. 392-94; Timmerman, *Promises*, pp. 80-87.
17. Ryskamp, "History," p. 191; Timmerman, *Promises*, pp. 92, 161.

part of faculty. The first scene in this act, however, featured a new round in the old debate over the purpose and character of Christian college education. From his experience as Calvin's wartime president, Henry Schultze worried about the technical, pragmatic emphases that would come with governmental aid to education, but the war veteran and new faculty star, Henry Zylstra of the English department, thought the threat lay closer to home. It was Christian Reformed people themselves who hungered for the practical, who would indulge a prettified version of mass culture, who wished to join good pay with inner piety and call it a Christian life. B. K. Kuiper's old charge of sanctified materialism was here reborn, and so were both his solutions. On the one hand Zylstra sounded the themes of integrative Calvinism, of world- and life-views lending coherence to education, substance to religion, and glory to God. On the other hand he pitched the contest as mind over nature, art over technique, and elite over popular culture. Not that he endorsed high culture as such; no, every work was to be scrutinized for its motive mind and tested by Christian measure. But the works worth the scrutiny were the classics. In wrestling with these, students would develop a worthier Christianity than Seceder squeamishness and a worthier mind than pop sentimentality. Zylstra's targets, the pious tract and pulp fiction, he deemed to be soul mates. So also his icons, Christianity and "mind." Kuyperianism and Idealism embraced.[18]

The monitors out in the denomination had nothing against good taste but they did worry about entangling alliances. The one they first suspected was political, namely, the protest of a dozen Calvin faculty members against the denominational magazine's endorsement of Red-baiting and, implicitly (the year was 1951), McCarthyism. The paper's editor, the Reverend Henry J. Kuiper, had led the attack on the college in 1921, had pushed the investigation of 1939, and now once more had the pleasure of exacting a penitent apology from the faculty as a body.[19] The theological winds were up, too. In 1951 virtually the whole Calvin Seminary faculty was

18. Henry Zylstra, *Testament of Vision* (Grand Rapids: Eerdmans, 1958).
19. Stob, "CRC Schools," pp. 394-95; Timmerman, *Promises*, pp. 110-11, 185-93.

replaced for having quarreled themselves to an impasse. One of the temporary replacements was Cornelius Van Til, a former student of Jellema, who had exchanged his teacher's positive Calvinism for the antithetical sort. The same year H. Evan Runner, converted to Kuyperianism while a student of Van Til at Westminster Theological Seminary, was hired in the college's philosophy department.[20]

For the first time in thirty years antithetical Calvinists had a central place in the Calvin circle, and they enjoyed it. They railed against Jellema's "synthesis" of Christianity with Plato, against Zylstra's "confusion" of theology with aesthetics, against the "dualistic" positing of spirit over nature, instead of spirit against spirit, as the essential contest of culture. They scorned dull conformity and flaccid materialism fully as much as did their opponents, only with cutting invective. If their style attracted few among the in-crowd, it thrilled the marginal and outcast — first of all, youth from the postwar Dutch immigration to Canada, but also the native-born raised on and revolting against American culture religion.[21] Those it did not attract were often stimulated to work toward an adequate retort. Thus, the divisions of the early 1950s stimulated intellectual intensity and recommitted all parties involved to the common heritage over which they were quarreling. No one could get away with *just* good taste, scholarly excellence, Christian dogma, or American patriotism. Everyone scouted secularism despite its brilliant mind and fundamentalism despite its Christian warmth. Everyone could join Harry Jellema in renewing Calvin's quest for a third way, for "education and scholarship that shall be wholly and vitally expressive of the Christian faith, that shall be of the highest academic quality, and that shall be *both at once.*" Or as Henry Zylstra put it amid the battles of 1951: "Our schools must be schools — that for one thing. And then they must be Christian — that for another thing. And in making these two points I shall want to insist, of course, that they must be both at once."[22]

The quarreling also dimmed because two new ventures were

---

20. Timmerman, *Promises,* pp. 189-91; Bratt, *Dutch Calvinism,* pp. 190-96.
21. Bratt, *Dutch Calvinism,* pp. 195-96, 208-10.
22. William Harry Jellema, quoted in Ryskamp, "History," p. 334; Zylstra, *Testament,* p. 90.

demanding attention. In the CRC's centennial year, 1957-58, when questions of "whence and whither" were thick in the air, the college administration began unveiling plans for a huge new campus on the edge of town, and Harry Jellema published a detailed critique of the college curriculum and a proposal for its replacement. The physical relocation began in 1962 and took ten years; the curricular reform went into planning in 1963 and was accomplished in five.[23] Thus, Calvin overhauled its two fundamental structures at the same time — simultaneously with the greatest decade of campus upheaval in American history. The Providence that attended the college's fledging in the 1920s now returned for its revamping.

The need for more space was the main reason Calvin moved its campus. College expansion after World War II had tapped all the capacity of the Franklin Street site but had still proved inadequate; the new site was some twenty times larger than the old. An unintended consequence became clear when the long-contemplated move took place during a time of increased racial turmoil. Leaving the section of the city that was rapidly becoming predominantly African-American lent apparent plausibility to accusation of "white flight." Even though this was not true as to motive, some people associated with the college did feel relief at getting out of what was called "a changing neighborhood." And so it happened, English professor John J. Timmerman recounted, that just as the inner city heated up and students cried for involvement, just when 1960s' passions flamed and students demanded relevance, Calvin students found themselves transplanted to the pastoral isolation of Knollcrest Farm.[24] As wheezing buses shuttled students back and forth between the two campuses, the college itself seemed in suspension, trying to transplant a history that had fought to maintain a Dutch Calvinism in America into a future where Christianity was to transform America.

To change the world, Calvin decided first to change its own curriculum. The reform owed something to the academic climate of the time, as was evident from the new plan's provision of a pass-fail

---

23. W. Harry Jellema, "The Curriculum in a Liberal Arts College" (Grand Rapids: Calvin College, 1958); Timmerman, *Promises*, pp. 144, 164.

24. Timmerman, *Promises*, pp. 144-48.

January Interim term for experimental courses. But the change owed far more to the college's own tradition. From the start Calvin had insisted it would not be a regular college with chapel and Bible courses added on, but in fact the curriculum it had adopted in 1921 was imported en bloc from the University of Michigan — with Bible and theology courses added on. Even worse, Harry Jellema noted, Michigan had then just finished remodeling its curriculum to the fashion set by Charles Eliot at Harvard, meaning that Calvin's curricular structure derived from the dictates of scientific, evolutionary naturalism.[25] Thus the reformers of the 1960s could make fundamental changes in radical times by invoking orthodoxy.

The new plan, published as *Christian Liberal Arts Education (CLAE)*, clearly articulated how a college curriculum might be structured from Reformed premises about the integrality of all life, learning, and faith. *CLAE* instituted a "disciplinary" model of education in which "teachers and students together [would] engag[e] in the various scholarly disciplines, directed and enlightened in their inquiries by the Word of God." This education was still to have a clear liberal arts purpose of "disinterested" study rather than immediately usable knowledge; the college's historic rejection of pragmatism continued. But *CLAE* also rejected "classical" curricular models as overemphasizing intellectual history and elite culture.[26] Instead it valorized each discipline as equal in dignity or possibility, consonant with Kuyper's reminder that Christ was Lord over *all* and quite in contrast to Harry Jellema's 1958 proposal that would have made the sciences handmaids to the humanities. *CLAE*, further, resisted the tides of academic specialization by requiring a large core and relatively fewer courses in the major, a breadth-over-depth approach that accorded well with Kuyperian worldview construction. This was also evident in the expectation that both the core course in each discipline and every major as a whole reflect upon their grounds and procedures in light of Christian beliefs and norms. Attention to disciplinary practices, in turn, pointed to the keystone

25. Jellema, "Curriculum," p. 5.
26. Calvin College Curriculum Study Committee, *Christian Liberal Arts Education* (Grand Rapids: Calvin College/Eerdmans, 1970), pp. 40-47; quotation at p. 47.

of the new curriculum. Learning was not to take place for its own sake but to serve the Lord by prompting action in the world. Here, neither Abraham Kuyper nor John Calvin was the real inspiration so much as H. Richard Niebuhr. His *Christ and Culture* served as scripture for "Christian Perspectives on Learning," a first-year interdisciplinary course deemed vital to the new curriculum; and his fifth category, "Christ transforming culture," effectively became the college's new motto.

Curricular reform went on without much outside interest, but by the time of its implementation in the late 1960s, the watchmen on the walls of the CRC Zion could only wonder what was transforming what. Better, they did not wonder at all but were certain — and appalled. In this they were one with millions across the land, only with a distinctive twist. There were no riots at Calvin, though some demonstrations; no obstruction of the campus, though a few faculty-approved moratoria to mark Earth Day or allow antiwar protests. Students did not always behave like ladies and gentlemen, though some faculty deemed them, in retrospect, the most inquisitive they have encountered in their entire careers. To part of the CRC constituency, however, all these considerations, good or ill, paled next to the issue of movie-going. As late as 1962-63 the editors of *Chimes,* the student newspaper, had been censured for reviewing Ingmar Bergman films shown at a local theater. Although feeling compelled to enforce the rules, Calvin President William Spoelhof noted that the editors had been motivated by a Calvinist mandate, the "concern about our broad cultural obligations as Christians living in the world."[27] Then, the 1966 Synod reversed the CRC's historic position by stating that "the film arts are a legitimate cultural medium to be used by the Christian in the same way that every cultural medium is to be used."[28] The next year a student-

27. Board of Trustees minutes, "Student Publications," Article 43R, May 23, 1963, Calvin College Archives; quoted in David Larsen, "Evangelical Christian Higher Education, Culture and Social Conflict" (unpublished Ph.D. dissertation, Loyola University of Chicago, 1992), p. 91. The part of this dissertation pertaining to Calvin College was of considerable help in mapping (changes in) student life there since 1960.

28. *Acts of Synod of the Christian Reformed Church, 1966* (Grand Rapids: Christian Reformed Publishing House, 1966), p. 200.

faculty committee was constituted as the Calvin Film Council and began a regular program of showing movies on campus.

In all this maneuvering the putative cultural qualities of film were obscured by its symbolic status to all parties. To conservative constituents, *the* moral boundary between holiness and worldliness had been erased. The college administration thought that moderation was now to rule. Student reformers-turned-radicals were determined that it would not. Paul Schrader, later a premier film director and screen writer *(Taxi Driver, Last Temptation of Christ)*, was, as a student, rejected four times in his applications to serve on the film program. He went on to full martyrdom when he and the rest of the *Chimes* staff lost their positions in 1968 on allegations of bad taste, insubordination, and misuse of funds. Perhaps the film issue was an apt symbol after all, for over the next two years protests against dorm hours, mandatory chapel, the Vietnam war, American racism, environmental degradation, and more all swirled around the buildings where movies now were shown and on the *Chimes* pages where Schrader had ruled.

The tumult came to a head in April 1970. On the heels of the United States's invasion of Cambodia, the college gave students place to picket and speak at the Spring convocation, observed the first Earth Day, and witnessed the greatest crisis of William Spoelhof's twenty-five-year presidency. But the third had nothing to do with the first or the second. Perhaps pathetically, perhaps absurdly, but in any case tellingly, the crisis occurred over the *Chimes*'s annual mock issue, which that year targeted not campus foibles but the CRC's weekly magazine, the *Banner*. That the student editors' disciplinary hearing was interrupted by news of the shootings at Kent State University demonstrated how great was the distance, still, between Calvin's world and the one outside.

*   *   *

Administrators and constituents may have feared, and student leaders anticipated, the 1970-71 academic year as the dawn of further radicalism and disruption. Yet that year was one of almost eerie calm. Student leaders turned to new interests, and the college as a whole returned to face historic questions in its markedly

changed environment. The 1970s was a time when Calvin sought
to replace faltering formulas, structurally and ideologically.

The first revision came in the student recruitment system. For
its entire history Calvin had relied upon denominational mechanisms to deliver it students, and the system had worked. Each year
the college could expect a fixed yield of the CRC's age-eligible youth.
But the system and the demographic pool slipped simultaneously
in the early 1970s: enrollment fell from 3,575 in 1968 to 3,185 in
1972. After straining to build the new campus, the college now
faced a prospect of empty desks. Both out of necessity and of the
conviction that it had much to offer Christians beyond the CRC,
Calvin undertook its first venture outside the ethnic-denomi-
national fold by recruiting in evangelical Protestant circles. By and
large the initiative worked. Enrollments broke the 4,000 mark in
1980 and peaked at 4,505 in 1988, with the percentages coming
from CRC background (still around 90 in 1970) dipping to 72 and
65 respectively.

This success had its costs, of course. One has been the increased
level of uncertainty regarding each year's enrollment, a particularly
acute concern at an institution whose budget is 85 percent tuition-
driven and where refusing to cap the size of entering classes is an
article of faith. Faculty, facility, and budget planning have therefore
been chained to the roller coaster of enrollment vagaries: 4,108 in
1980 became 3,828 in 1982; 4,505 in 1988 fell to 3,725 in 1990.
Another cost has come in increased pressure for student retention.
Calvin's tradition of virtually open admissions had always been
balanced by a process of honest or heartless (depending on the
source) excisions, typically exercised on first-year students by self-
appointed faculty commissars of quality control. Any tilt toward
toleration or second chances could threaten the college's academic
quality, just as any perceived tilt could lower faculty morale. Finally,
recruitment and retention have required more staff, more faculty
energies, and continuous nuancing of the campus image.

Nor did administration grow only on these counts. Along
with other colleges and universities, Calvin saw staff numbers
increase over the '70s and '80s at a rate far higher than the
faculty's, with the result that by the late 1980s the latter fell below
the former for the first time in the college's history. Tellingly, the

college's administration building, named after William Spoelhof, was dubbed the "college center." On the original campus design that title belonged to the trinity of library-classroom building, chapel, and college-denominational archive clustered together on Knollcrest's high ground to symbolize past and future, faith and reason, intersecting in the present.[29] The elevation of the administrative "center" in their place might be taken as a sad tale of bureaucratization except that, in architectural fact, the college has no center. The campus is rather a tasteful arrangement of pods quite reflective of the department-centric curriculum and the divisionally directed co-curriculum that define how the college actually functions. Two rhetorical sinews tie all these together: positively, the dedication of all parties to solid Christian higher education; negatively, the complaint that faculty rarely see members of other departments nor administrators of any division nor students outside of class. The integrity of the positive bond has always depended on Calvin's being an integral community; the worry about the contrary bespeaks a significant challenge.

Increased differentiation is thus one hallmark of Calvin's past quarter century. Another is suggested by the transit from "professorial" to "professional" as the overriding tone of college life. While teaching undergraduates remains their primary work, the faculty over the last twenty-five years have shown a marked increase in commitment to research, publication, and related artistic and professional endeavors. Under the leadership of President Anthony Diekema, more funding for research was provided, especially in a program called Calvin Research Fellowships. Coupled with a strong sabbatical program, this initiative distinguishes Calvin in terms of support for research. At the same time, the expectation of scholarship has left many faculty feeling significant tension between the investments in time and energy required for research and the continuing demands of teaching, advising, and community service. Department and discipline have come to rival college in defining primary loyalties. This became especially noteworthy in the 1980s as Calvin had to compete, with only modest success, with major research universities for the services of its best-known scholars.

29. Ryskamp, "History," p. 309.

The trend toward professionalization affected governance as well. A new policy-making structure heavy on faculty committees was instituted in the late 1960s on the heels of the campus and curricular changes, but its impact took longer to play out. In theory the FOSCO (Faculty Organization Study Committee) plan installed broader and more effective power in the faculty by subdividing responsibilities that formerly had preoccupied the body as a whole and by subjecting administrative fiat to regular faculty review. In practice the reorganization vitiated the faculty meeting as a deliberative body, turning it into a virtual rubber stamp for committee decisions. And increased complexity within the administration submerged effective decision-making on some issues of long-term community significance in the toils of divisional structures. In short, the more concrete detail the faculty have had to deal with in committee, the less philosophical discussion they have been able to carry on as a body. This development has meshed with the style that Anthony Diekema brought to the college presidency in 1976. While Spoelhof was caricatured as a benevolent monarch, Diekema was viewed by many as a manager whose favorite word was "process." He frankly told the college at his arrival that he was not a visionary but one to implement the vision of others, particularly the faculty. Through no necessary fault of his, however, the coherence of faculty vision and the mechanisms for its expression have lessened in the past twenty years.

Professionalization was also a key ingredient in the main curricular change of the Diekema administration. In the early 1970s a special faculty committee produced a report that suggested moving the college from "liberal arts monism" to "liberal arts centrism." To die-hards of such "monism" the notion had all the charm of the report's acronym: *PECLAC (Professional Education and the Christian Liberal Arts College)*.[30] The report self-consciously stood on the shoulders of the previous decade's *Christian Liberal Arts Education* and, at the hands of its principal writer, philosophy professor Richard Mouw, aimed to flesh out the neo-Kuyperian concerns of that document. Theologically, *PECLAC* argued that since all of life

30. Calvin College Professional Programs Committee, "Professional Education and the Christian Liberal Arts College," February 9, 1973.

is corrupted by sin and so needs to be redeemed, there is no subject unworthy of study in a Christian college. Historically, it noted that Calvin was not just now beginning professional programs but had offered these from the start, in fact had taken two of these — pre-seminary and teacher education — as its original *raison d'être*. Qualitatively, the report did not open the door to any and every field but set forward criteria compatible with liberal arts interests for determining acceptability.

The ensuing years brought success down this track, and unease around it. Students voted with their feet for new programs in accountancy, social work, criminal justice, recreation, and nursing, while already extant programs in engineering and especially business expanded greatly. By the late 1980s the numbers of students graduating in professional programs would outnumber those in traditional liberal arts disciplines. The *PECLAC* curriculum thus probably equalled the new recruiting strategy in bolstering enrollment. But many wondered about the cost of this success, too. Preparing preachers and teachers — the old pre-professionalism — clearly carried on the usual purposes of liberal arts education; the new programs were more ambiguous on that score. *PECLAC* had advocated a curricular move from "liberal arts monism" to "liberal arts centrism." Upon the eve of his departure for Fuller Seminary, *PECLAC* author Richard Mouw warned that the many new programs threatened just that liberal arts center and with it the vitality of the collegiate enterprise.[31]

If the liberal arts classroom has felt rivalled in this era, so has the classroom as such. The student-affairs division has grown in staff and confidence to claim a mission of providing the "co-curriculum" of college life. This venture, too, claims Kuyperian warrant. If "all of life" falls under Christ's Lordship, then surely the majority of their time that Calvin students spend outside the classroom must be claimed and redeemed. Besides, recruitment and retention imperatives demanded programming congruent with this effort, as do student perceptions that college is now an entitlement — as before 1970 it was a privilege — of middle-class

31. Comments by Mouw in a meeting of the Calvin faculty, heard by the authors.

status. Dorm room and classroom, gymnasium and library on this view can all become feeding stations in the smorgasbord of the college "experience" that one passes through between parental home and finding a job.

Managing these mandates required another, equally innovative professionalization. The oversight of student life on Calvin's campus had usually been left to sanctified amateurs. There was no counselling center and only lately a chaplain. Authority figures in the residence halls were not trained specifically for the job, and many qualified because they were widowed mothers. This, too, changed around 1970. The Broene Counselling Center now has five professionally trained staff; the vice-president for student affairs and the deans of student life are well credentialed in human services delivery. The chaplain carries on a wide-ranging ministry, and residence hall directors have replaced the widowed moms, bringing along concepts of community building learned in graduate schools. Indeed, a lovely paradox is the genuine concern that many of the student-affairs staff have for "the whole person," a clear echo of the Kuyperian notions of the faculty who sometimes look dourly on their doings. At the same time the campus religious ethos, set less by the voluntary (since 1970) chapel program than by dorm and interest-group Bible studies, indicates some drift toward a piety that drafts off both the old Seceder impulses and movements in the CRC toward models of fundamentalistic evangelicalism. This account of structural changes indicates a ready, if at times ironic, consensus in place around Kuyperian ideology. Such a consensus was never complete nor quickly achieved, nor have its notions been as clearly directive as its proponents had hoped. Yet since 1975 a Kuyperianism at once chastened and cheerful has held sway over the college's rhetoric and action, put there by the same person who designed the new curriculum, Nicholas Wolterstorff. His triumph was all the more notable for being announced in what had been the den of the enemy. Ever since the early 1950s' battles between philosophers Evan Runner and Cornelius Van Til on the one hand and Harry Jellema and Henry Stob on the other, the Kuyperian cause had been divided — sometimes with real animosity — between the "antitheticals" and the "progressives." It was as heir to the latter that Wolterstorff in 1975 ventured into the bastion of the former, the Institute for Christian Studies in Toronto, to offer an accord.[32]

The offer exacted a high price. The antitheticals (or Dooye-weeerdians, as they called themselves after the Dutch legal philosopher Herman Dooyeweerd) first had to give up their claims that God's "law-word," embedded in the structures of creation, constituted a revelation equal to Scripture. "This understanding of the Word of God," Wolterstorff concluded, was "unacceptable as Christian theology." Second, he demystified the Dooyeweerdians' social philosophy of "sphere sovereignty." What was original in it, Wolterstorff insisted, came from Kuyper; what was ornate, from Dooyeweerd; what was true and useful — and much of it was, the speaker allowed — was to be so credited from experience, not from Scripture. What credit, then, belonged to the Dooyeweerdian party? A most important role, Wolterstorff answered: It had kept the CRC and Calvin College from a likely fall into fundamentalism; it had cultivated the Reformed heritage, pressing its claims against a flaccid accommodation to Americanism; and it stood ready to bring its zeal to the reinvigoration of the Kuyperian progressive wing.

Wolterstorff's lecture marked a fundamental turning in Calvin's postwar history. At one stroke he resolved the historic tensions between *all* the parties in the church. The pietists were glad to hear his affirmation that the definitive speech of God was in the Bible, not in creation. Those interested in Christian cultural critique now had the Kuyperian tradition accessible to them without the complex system of Dooyeweerd. Here was an insight, even a motto, that could be appropriated for the academic calling at Calvin College. Its integral view of all of life as response to God made plausible the assertion that chemistry, physics, biology, and mathematics have as much a place in the curriculum as theology, history, philosophy, and literature. Moreover, the guiding methodology for all these undertakings would be the desire to integrate Christian faith with learning in a particular discipline. Later on, the Christian College Coalition would also take up these notions as its reason for being. While other traditions contribute to the Coalition's ideology, it is

32. Nicholas Wolterstorff, "The AACS in the CRC: Will It Guide Us or Divide Us?" *The Banner,* January 3, 1975, pp. 13-15; January 10, 1975, pp. 18-20.

this line in the Reformed tradition that has given the approach its real appeal to evangelicals. On the other hand, while closely associated with Calvin College, this approach came to dominance there only a little before its spread elsewhere. Put another way, the ideology had been around in Dutch Reformed thinking for about a century but surely as a minority view. Only after 1975 did it become a vision for all seasons.

Yet, this story of ideological development is not complete without mentioning an alternative mission statement that has gone largely unheeded. While the Kuyperian "worldview" approach was still rising in evangelical circles, a number of critics emerged, especially amid Wesleyan/holiness and Mennonite circles, complaining of its static and all-too-academic character. On this view Reformed ideology is too long on principles and too short on practice.

The same critique emerged at Calvin College itself, once again from Nicholas Wolterstorff. This time, however, Calvin gave the local prophet only the honor of a polite hearing, and that second-hand, for this critique was first offered at the 1982 inauguration of Richard Chase as president of Wheaton College.[33] However much cited at other institutions, Wolterstorff's proposal for a "third stage" in Christian higher education has been little heeded on his home ground.

Wolterstorff's points were both easy to comprehend and difficult to make operational. There were two stages, the author suggested, that characterized Wheaton's history, and a third stage toward which it should aspire. Stage I was characterized by the evangelical withdrawal from culture and society following the loss of face in the fundamentalist-modernist controversy. Stage II was characterized by the re-emergence of confidence in the years after World War II, when neo-evangelicalism rose from fundamentalism's ashes. Its main theme was engagement with culture, not withdrawal from it, a theme whose touchstone phrase was "the integration of faith and learning." Wolterstorff was gracious enough not to stress the Reformed roots of integrative educational theories. He nevertheless noted that "Christ and culture" issues had become the staple products of the Christian College Coalition.

33. Nicholas Wolterstorff, "The Mission of the Christian College at the End of the 20th Century," *Reformed Journal*, June 1983, pp. 14-18.

For Stage III Wolterstorff asked Wheaton — and other leading Christian colleges — to move from a consideration of Christ and culture to the church in society. Just as there was no disembodied "Christ" outside the real life of the churches, so "culture" devoid of its social location was at least feckless, and probably sterile. What Wolterstorff called for was a collegiate commitment to social transformation. This would, the author insisted, require Christian colleges to change both ethos and curriculum; ethos insofar as it invoked a sense of holy unease with society as it was disordered by, for example, nationalism and capitalism; curriculum insofar as it needed to change from the disciplinary structures that the same author had advocated in *Christian Liberal Arts Education* to programs in "peace and war, nationalism, poverty, urban ugliness, ecology, crime and punishment."[34] Calvin College has made some new efforts in off-campus programs in this direction but otherwise has shown little inclination to move much beyond the "faith and learning" consensus of Stage II.

*   *   *

Internally, then, Calvin over the past twenty-five years has felt the conundrum of quantitative growth on every count set off by diffusion in organization and ethos. The paradox mounts in light of Calvin's unprecedented visibility on the national scene during these same years as a model of Christian higher education. *U.S. News* rates it high for students, the secular academy notes its distinctive angle, and the Christian College Coalition follows its example of faith-learning integration. Calvin has won these roles, particularly the latter, because, just as the CRC has opened up to the evangelical Protestant world, so the evangelical world has arrived historically at the point that Dutch Neo-Calvinism might have been the first to discern. Taking just Abraham Kuyper's dicta about perspectival scholarship, he sounds postmodern. Taking his dicta about the continuing salience of creation and the universal Lordship of Christ, he legitimates for Christians the study of every person, place, and thing on earth — and he warrants study, the academic life, as fully as good a Christian calling as the "full-time Christian service" American evangelicals

34. Ibid., p. 18.

have ritually praised. Taking seriously his combined stress upon principle and pluralism, Calvin College has become fit for articulating credible Christian conviction in a postmodern world. In earnestly applying principle across all domains of campus life while blending and intertwining these with Dutch, or immigrant, hardheaded practicality, Calvin has become a proven, workable enterprise.

This enterprise has proven not only workable but one that has gained a recognition in North American religious and academic culture that was nearly unimaginable two generations ago. In the whole growth of evangelical scholarship, Calvin College has exercised a leadership disproportionate to its size and history. For example, the Calvin Center for Christian Scholarship (CCCS) was founded in 1977 under the lead of President Diekema, with provisions for an ample endowment. The CCCS has sponsored some thirty research teams (a majority of whose members have come from outside of Calvin) in producing books and articles that have signaled not only the possibility but the desirability of perspectival scholarship. Several of the CCCS books have had considerable impact. Indeed, the entire question of how to work out a Christian perspective in a given discipline was new to most evangelicals, thus allowing Calvin people the opportunity of being given the lead. This can be most pointedly seen in the perspectival series "Through the Eyes of Faith," sponsored by the Christian College Coalition and published by Harper Collins. The series offers accessible supplementary texts to be used in beginning courses in the various liberal arts disciplines. When the Coalition wanted a person to head the series, they chose Nicholas Wolterstorff. When writers were needed, the Coalition again went disproportionally to Calvin people, for example, Susan Gallagher for the literature volume, Shirley Roels for the business book, and Ronald Wells for the history volume. Further, when Christian organizations within academic disciplines were formed (e.g., the Society of Christian Philosophers, the Conference on Faith and History, the Conference on Christianity and Literature, Christians in Political Science), Calvin College professors were once more in the lead. In sum, this remarkable record of leadership, though sometimes arousing resentment among evangelical institutions, was a natural outreach for scholars in a college committed to Kuyperian-principled learning and scholarship. If others wish to emulate Calvin in this regard, the college will take it as a sign of divine blessing.

Providence is still deft enough, however, to keep the college from pure joy. Calvin College is perennially as anxious as was its namesake, and with good reason. The historical record shows that Calvinism, despite or because of claiming all the world so insistently for God, has been one of the West's great engines of secularization. In academic life in particular, as former Calvin history professor George Marsden has written, secularization occurs not necessarily when religion becomes too little but when it becomes so much and so broad that it is robbed of content.[35] It was not craven atheists who engineered the secularization of the major American universities but those purveyors of religion whose parameters were so broad that, like Holmes's "Wonderful One Hoss Shay," they just broke one day, for reasons that no one could fully explain. In Calvin's case, setting all aspects of campus life under Kuyperian principle may also have made that principle flaccid, while teaching and writing from a distinctively Christian slant does not always produce as distinctive or as predictable a result as had been imagined.

The story herein of Calvin College has been a degendered and deracinated one. Yet over the past twenty-five years in the North American academy, surely one of the greatest insights has been that we are not merely humans in general but that gender and race matter to our particularity. Calvin College was, in fact, fairly slow to respond to the challenges of racial and gender equity. While the faculty is still predominantly male and white, and the student body overwhelmingly white, Calvin has made some progress toward diversity. Moreover, the college has resources that draw upon its strengths that will, we hope, yield results in the future. The faculty is solidly behind the desire for a more diverse student body. As early as 1971 the faculty initiated a move, later adopted by the administration, to actively recruit persons from the North American racial minority communities. Further, in 1985 the faculty passed a document in which President Diekema was personally involved; on matters of race, the college faculty and staff would be enriched by colleagues from minority

35. George M. Marsden, *The Soul of the American University* (New York: Oxford University Press, 1994).

communities. As to gender, a special task force in 1991 issued an important report on "the chilly climate for women" at Calvin College. The report resulted in a plan to implement gender equity. There were administrators in place by the early 1990s to oversee matters specifically related to race and gender, and to making Calvin a more comprehensive and diverse Christian institution.

Yet at the end of 120 years, with all the shifts of scene and slant, Calvin finds itself close to where it started under Gerrit Boer. It is still *"onze school,"* a CRC venture, only the denomination is now filled with prosperous members who cannot regard themselves as despised of the world, or reject it in return. The college still looks out at nearby traffic today, though not at the railroad but at a major highway that runs right past the campus. Along that road to the north lie mega-churches, one Christian Reformed in title but little distinguishable from the other, undenominational fundamentalist giant it emulates. Over against evangelicalism's recent rise in numbers and public visibility, the distinctives of Calvinism that have given the CRC its glue and the college its edge seem less compelling to maintain. A mile south, the highway runs between two shopping malls, one West Michigan's largest. These were built simultaneously with the Knollcrest campus and provide Calvin with its greatest challenge. For they represent the kind of world that even pietist Seceders had a hard time resisting, as B. K. Kuiper and Henry Zylstra noted. Their proximity represents a magnetism more likely to transform the church and the college according to the culture than the opposite flow idealized by Kuyper and Niebuhr.

In 1995, Anthony Diekema honorably completed his twenty-year presidency. Chief on the agenda of his successor will be assessing the current status of Calvin's historic struggles: the first between two Christian attitudes toward culture, flight or transformation; the other between the commitments of Christianity and the culture of American materialism. It would be a cruel irony if the whole enterprise wound up halfway between the first pair as a mode of avoiding the second choice; that is, if Calvin turns out world-affirming enough to remain respectably middle class, world-denying enough to keep religion private, and worldly American enough to shop the mall without the guilt or anxiety that Calvinism has always thought the anteroom of conversion.

'Once More Unto the Breach, Dear Friends": Gender Studies and the Christian Academy

Susan Van Zanten Gallagher

Act three of William Shakespeare's *Henry V* opens with British invasion troops standing before the walls of the French city of Harfleur. The king, surrounded by fleeing soldiers carrying scaling ladders, urges his retreating force to try again in one of the more inspiring speeches in the Shakespearean canon: "Once more unto the breach, dear friends, once more, / Or close the wall up with our English dead!" Apparently Henry has led at least one previous sortie since there is a breach in the wall, an opening made by a break-through, a broken or torn place.

I would like to reflect on the breaches in gender studies in several different senses of the word.[1] In one sense, gender studies represents a scholarly breakthrough; an impressive amount of new information and new perspectives based on considerations of gender has emerged during the past two decades. Some scholars even argue that feminist thought has contributed to an intellectual revolution comparable to those produced by Copernicus, Darwin, and Freud.[2] While that may be an overstatement, I think there is no question, regardless of whether one approves of this phenome-non or not, that entire academic fields have changed shape.

---

1. All of the definitions of *breach* referred to in this essay are from *Webster's New World Dictionary*.
2. Carolyn Heilbrun, "Feminist Criticism in Departments of Literature," *Academe*, Sept.-Oct. 1983, p. 14.

Gifted but overlooked women poets, novelists, composers, and artists have been rediscovered; Chaucer, Shakespeare, and Milton are being read in new and provocative ways; therapeutic drugs are now tested on female as well as male bodies; historians have broadened their definition of history to include the more traditionally female-dominated realms of social life; psychologists are aware of the significance of analyzing data collected from adolescent girls instead of adolescent boys. Literature, art, music, sociology, political science, biology, medicine, history, and psychology have all undergone major changes. As Daphne Patai and Noretta Koertge state, "the use of gender as a powerful conceptual tool and a key category of analysis in the humanities and social sciences [has] transformed entire fields."[3]

These new openings in scholarship have not always been acknowledged or embraced by the Christian academy. Women and women's accomplishments still are often overlooked in our curriculum and scholarship. For example, when Elaine Storkey, a British Christian philosopher and social critic, began researching Scottish church history a few years ago, she was amazed to discover that if she were to believe the historical record, there were no women in Scotland between 1170 and 1928, except Mary Queen of Scots.[4] Her experience is reminiscent of that of Virginia Woolf, vainly paging through Trevelyan's *History of England* in search of information about women and finding little other than the fact that they were frequently "locked up, beaten and flung about the room."[5]

Mark Noll's otherwise excellent study of *The Scandal of the Evangelical Mind* contains a significant lacuna when it comes to gender issues in American church history, as Mary Stewart Van Leeuwen points out in a recent review.[6] Noll says little about the

3. Daphne Patai and Noretta Koertge, *Professing Feminism: Cautionary Tales from the Strange World of Women's Studies* (New York: Basic Books, 1994), p. 2.
4. Elaine Storkey, "The Hidden History of Women in the Church," lecture given at Calvin College, Grand Rapids, Mich., 12 March 1991.
5. Virginia Woolf, *A Room of One's Own* (1929; New York: Harcourt Brace Jovanovich, 1957), p. 45.
6. Mary Stewart Van Leeuwen, "The Scandal of the (Male) Evangelical Mind," paper presented at the Third Annual Crossroads Conference on Faith and Public Policy, July 1995.

significant intellectual contributions of evangelical women to the abolitionist and suffragist movements, does not consider the impact of gender on revivalism or fundamentalism, and fails to take into account the well-documented nineteenth-century "feminization of American culture" in his analysis.[7] Similarly, in the comprehensive history of Calvin College originally prepared by Ronald Wells and James Bratt for a Lilly Foundation study, we find no mention of when women were first admitted to Calvin (it was in 1902) or any discussion of the many changes that must have taken place during the years in which Calvin moved from being a male academy to an institution that is now over 50 percent female.[8]

The Christian academy too often forgets to think about women or to take account of gender in its scholarship and teaching. We sometimes fail to respond to or even acknowledge the recent transformations in scholarship. Given the controversies over gender within evangelicalism in general and within particular denominations, including the Christian Reformed Church, perhaps we can understand this omission. But if we fail to address gender issues in our institutional structures, pedagogy, and curriculum, at the very least, we are failing to prepare our students adequately for either the gender-conscious society of which they are a part or for the academic world that many will encounter in graduate studies.

Even more compelling, however, for scholars who believe it is our responsibility to study, in Abraham Kuyper's famous phrase, "every square inch of creation," is the reality that the realm of

7. The definitive study appears in Ann Douglas, *The Feminization of American Culture* (New York: Alfred A. Knopf, 1978). For other important works that consider the impact of gender in American social and church history, see Nancy F. Cott, *The Bonds of Womanhood: "Women's Sphere" in New England, 1780-1835* (New Haven: Yale University Press, 1978); Janette Hassey, *No Time for Silence: Evangelical Women in Public Ministry around the Turn of the Century* (Grand Rapids: Zondervan, 1986); Margaret Lamberts Bendroth, *Fundamentalism and Gender, 1875 to Present* (New Haven: Yale University Press, 1994).

8. James D. Bratt and Ronald A. Wells, "Piety and Progress: A History of Calvin College," in Richard T. Hughes and William B. Adrian, eds., *Models for Christian Higher Education: Strategies for Survival and Success in the Twenty-first Century* (Grand Rapids: Eerdmans, 1997). A revised version of this essay, which includes a discussion of gender in Calvin's recent history, was presented at the inauguration and is included in this volume.

gender differences makes up many square inches. In the creation account found in the first chapter of Genesis, the fact that humanity is divided into male and female is the second thing that we learn about human beings, right after the fact that God created us in God's image. If we are to study, engage, and claim *all* of God's creation, gender should be a key component of our task. We need boldly to enter the opening caused by the breakthrough in gender studies.

There is a second kind of breach in gender studies today, however: a breach within the field itself, a breaking up, or division. Consider the titles of some influential recent publications, all by self-professed feminists: *Who Stole Feminism? How Women Have Betrayed Women*, by Christina Hoff Sommers; *Professing Feminism: Cautionary Tales from the Strange World of Women's Studies*, by Daphne Patai and Noretta Koertge. One section of Naomi Wolf's recent bestseller *Fire With Fire* is called "What Went Wrong? How So Many Women and Their Movement Parted Ways." Some idealistic feminists (which a Reformed feminist can never be) believe that the divisions chronicled in works such as these are a breach in yet a third sense: an infraction, the failure to observe a promise. For these idealists, the utopian feminist promise of unity and harmony has been rudely shattered by dissenting voices.

Let us consider some of the divisions that have arisen within gender studies. These breaches embody tensions that the Christian academy, in my opinion, would do well to note and to embrace, as is the theme for the celebration of President Byker's inauguration. Of course these divisions in gender studies are just one more aspect of what has been termed the "culture war" raging in contemporary American society. In that war, Christian scholars should not simply enter the fray on one side or another, nor defensively retreat from the battle, but move beyond it, assessing both the breaches and the solid defenses of all the contestants.

In so doing we might follow in some respects the lead of Gerald Graff, professor of English at the University of Chicago, who has been urging American academics to move — in the title of his recent book — "beyond the culture wars." Graff's pacification plan? "The best solution to today's conflicts over culture is to teach the conflicts themselves, making them part of our object of study and using them as a new kind of organizing principle to give the curriculum the clarity and focus that almost all sides now agree it lacks."[9] I will come back to this idea of teaching the conflicts and other ways that the Christian academy might engage gender studies, but first I want to examine the nature of the breach.

One of the many contested issues is the very term used to describe the field. Although some writers distinguish, in differing ways depending on their discipline, between *gender studies* and *women's studies*, I will use these terms interchangeably to refer to interdisciplinary academic programs that use gender as a category of analysis. Most programs are, in fact, called *women's studies*, and the primary professional organization in the field is called the National Women's Studies Association. Several programs located at Christian colleges, however, in an attempt to acknowledge that the study of gender includes both males and females, use the term *gender studies*, such as the minors at Eastern College and Wheaton College. (Wheaton's minor is, in a rather strange conflation, called Gender and Ethnic Studies.)

Other programs, such as the minor at Messiah College and my own institution's newly established minor, use the term *women's studies* as an attempt to provide truth in advertising. For in practical terms, these programs tend to focus on women and women's issues, because previous work has overlooked or ignored women. For example, Carol Gilligan was one of the first psychologists to point out that theories of moral development had been formed by researchers who studied male adolescents exclusively. What would happen, she asked, if the sample groups were female? Would the results differ? Her work on the moral development of females, while having its own methodological problems, demonstrated that previous supposedly gender-neutral research was, in fact, limited to one sex. By focusing on women, Gilligan also opened up a new understanding of men.[10]

Women's studies emerged in the 1970s as a by-product of the

9. Gerald Graff, *Beyond the Culture Wars: How Teaching the Conflicts Can Revitalize American Education* (New York: W. W. Norton, 1992), p. 12.

10. Carol Gilligan, *In a Different Voice: Psychological Theory and Women's Development* (Cambridge: Harvard University Press, 1982).

Second Wave of American feminism. Consequently, the divisions that exist in academic women's studies often mirror divisions in the general phenomenon of feminism. One way of discussing these tensions is provided by Naomi Wolf, who distinguishes between *victim feminism* and *power feminism*. Victim feminism, Wolf says, describes women as powerless but mystically good and nurturing, and stresses the evil done to women as a way to petition for their rights. It focuses on abuse, oppression, marginalization. Power feminism, on the other hand, "sees women as human beings . . . no better or worse than their male counterparts" and stresses the need for equality on the grounds of justice. It focuses on the recent impressive achievements of women and admits that women, too, sometimes dominate or exploit others. Wolf believes that the majority of American women have become estranged from the feminist movement because it has emphasized victimization rather than power. We have more power than we think, she tells women, hoping that her book will help to "consolidate the clout of the unlabeled resurgence of power feminism that has already rocked our world."[11]

Wolf's opposition of victim feminists and power feminists is similar to Christina Hoff Sommers's analysis of the breach between *gender feminists* and *equity feminists*. Gender feminists, Sommers says, believe that the oppression of women is a structural feature of our society and foster a "feminism of resentment" that focuses on the "collective guilt" of all men.[12] Equity feminists, on the other hand, embrace "the traditional, classically liberal, humanistic feminism . . . initiated more than 150 years ago" that focuses on equal political and educational opportunities for women.[13] The gender feminists, Sommers claims, have "stolen" feminism from the equity feminists, often by means of distorting and even manufacturing false data and evidence.

Sommers locates the headquarters of this conspiracy in the

11. Naomi Wolf, *Fire with Fire: The New Female Power and How It Will Change the 21st Century* (New York: Random House, 1993), pp. xvii, xix.
12. Christina Hoff Sommers, *Who Stole Feminism? How Women Have Betrayed Women* (New York: Simon & Schuster, 1994), pp. 16, 43-44.
13. Ibid., p. 22.

academy, claiming, rather melodramatically, that "the failure to distinguish between the reasonable and just cause of equity feminism and its unreasonable, unjust, ideological sister — gender feminism" has been one of the principal reasons for the decline in American education.[14] Her attack bears a strong resemblance to the arguments of Patai and Koertge, whose recent critique of women's studies programs distinguishes between *liberal feminists* (good) and *identity feminists* (bad). Liberal feminists focus on human equality, while gender feminists focus on gender differences. Liberal feminists, the authors claim, have two legitimate academic objectives: (1) to find overlooked women in the fields of academic study, and (2) to make women's lives a focus of inquiry on a par with men's lives. Identity feminists are not content to stop there, however; they want "a radical reappraisal of all the assumptions and values found in traditional scholarship."[15] Furthermore, identity feminists privilege *feeling* over *intellect,* merely switching the positive and negative poles of the patriarchal stereotype.

The cumulative effect of all these victim, gender, and identity feminists, these critics assert, is a massive case of illiberal education in the over six hundred women's studies programs existing in the United States today. Women's studies programs, it is alleged, practice ideological policing, extol emotions over intellect, lack academic rigor, proselytize rather than teach, and foster a cult of anger, among other ills. *Professing Feminism* is full of horror stories of males in the classroom silenced and humiliated; of majors that allow almost half their credits to be earned in internships; of feminists who reject rationality, logic, and science in favor of women's intuition; of instructors whose primary goal appears to be to discredit heterosexuality. You have all heard these stories; I myself have heard similar tales from former students taking women's studies courses in graduate school.

These stories are indeed highly disturbing, but how representative are they of the state of women's studies? Sommers's book is highly anecdotal, and the authors of *Professing Feminism* base their conclusions on interviews with only thirty women, many of whom

14. Ibid., p. 53.
15. Patai and Koertge, *Professing Feminism,* p. 115.

decline to be identified by name, most of whom are unhappy with women's studies programs. Given the fact that there are over six hundred women's studies programs, this is a fairly small, and unscientifically selected, sample. Patai and Koertge themselves both personally experienced the pressure for conformity within the women's studies programs at their respective institutions, and they both left these programs. But in the national response to and debate over their book, many other professors and students claimed, "It's not like that at my institution!"[16]

Another critical study of women's studies programs appeared in *Mother Jones* in 1993. Its author, Karen Lehrman, more carefully notes, "Not every women's studies course suffers from these flaws. In fact, the rigor and perspective of individual programs and classes vary widely."[17] Perhaps not unsurprisingly, Lehrman found some of the most rigorous and thoughtful courses offered at small liberal arts colleges with a tradition of educating women, like Smith, and some of the most politicized courses at schools such as Berkeley and Dartmouth ("perhaps compensating for the school's macho image," she suggests). In response to Lehrman's article, Elizabeth Fox-Genovese, former director of women's studies at Emory University, writes, "that what she described exists, all of us who have had anything to do with women's studies know to be true, although it remains open to discussion whether it is true of all women's studies programs."[18] Anecdotal claims can be found on both sides. The true extent to which an extreme gender feminism dominates and distorts women's studies programs is an empirical question, one that can only be answered through substantial research.

Do women's studies programs by nature consist of the extreme identity politics of the gender feminists? How many problems arise because of the personality of people involved and how many are structural or functional? Two of the three discontented professors

16. An account of these responses appears in Daphne Patai, "What's Wrong with Women's Studies?" *Academe,* July-Aug. 1995, pp. 30-35.

17. Karen Lehrman, "Off Course," *Mother Jones,* Sept.-Oct. 1993, p. 47.

18. Elizabeth Fox-Genovese, "Women Studies II," *Mother Jones,* Nov.-Dec. 1993, p. 7.

who are quoted extensively in *Professing Feminism* attribute the difficulties to "the specific temperaments of this group of people," and believe that such behavior is not necessary feminist, but rather "just individual and group pathology."[19] Innate depravity raises its ugly head once again.

We can also examine the substance of the critiques to determine if we are facing a systemic problem or a good idea that has gone wrong through all-too-human behavior. Is there something inherent to the field of women's studies that prompts divisiveness, intolerance, and sloppy thinking? Do women's studies programs necessarily have to look like those described by Patai and Koertge? Anecdotal evidence about the failure of some women's studies programs is not an argument against all women's studies programs.

The three critiques that I have described (all, we should note, written for a popular audience) rely on simple binary oppositions to make their rhetorical point. But such a simplistic division masks the true variety in gender studies. It does work well rhetorically, creating a "them" and "us" mentality, and causing most readers, like myself, to side initially with the equity or liberal feminists. But on further reflection, I think, "Wait a minute; it's much more complicated than that!" Most scholarly accounts of feminism discriminate among some seven or eight different kinds.[20] Furthermore, the positions that the critics describe and the quotes they select as representative of contemporary feminism are often misleading and exaggerated. Particularly muddied thinking and distorted categorizing arise when writers such as Sommers equate *gender feminists* — those who examine the differences between men and women — with what is usually known as *radical feminists* — those who believe that gender is an absolute determiner of behavior and that women are innately superior.

Just because the linguist Deborah Tannen, for example, studies the different conversational styles of men and women, does not

19. Patai and Koertge, *Professing Feminism*, pp. 19-20.

20. See, e.g., the more nuanced and complex discussion of types of feminism in Mary Stewart Van Leeuwen et al., *After Eden: Facing the Challenge of Gender Reconciliation* (Grand Rapids: Eerdmans, 1993), pp. 44-70. A standard history appears in Rosemary Tong, *Feminist Thought: A Comprehensive Introduction* (Boulder, Colo.: Westview Press, 1989).

mean that she thinks either (1) all women must speak in these patterns, or (2) those styles more frequently used by women are necessarily better. In fact, Tannen explicitly and repeatedly states that she is describing "different *but equally valid* styles."[21] Yet Sommers claims that all gender feminists possess a "militant gynocentrism and misandrism."[22] Tannen does not hate men; she just thinks that most (not all) of them carry on a conversation differently than she does. (Individual personality, family patterns, and ethnic communities also affect conversational styles, she acknowledges.)

This tendency to divide feminists into two opposing camps does reflect some of the origins of feminism. Seventy-five years ago, when women were campaigning for the vote, they employed two different strategies. Some adhered to the nineteenth-century "Cult of True Womanhood," which held that women were more mentally weak, physically fragile, morally pure, and inherently domestic than men. Many people believed that such angelic beings would be defiled were they to enter the public realm of politics, but some suffragists turned the tables to argue that the moral superiority of women meant that they should be given the vote, for the stabilizing influence of women was needed to counteract the destructive materialism and corruption that riddled nineteenth-century society. The slogan of the Women's Christian Temperance Union — "For God and Home and Native Land" — thus symbolized these women's efforts to bring the purity associated with the home into the national arena.

But the nineteenth century also had feminists who, in their battle for the vote, drew on the same liberal political ideals that the Founding Fathers used to justify the American Revolution. Inspired by Mary Wollstonecraft's *A Vindication of the Rights of Women* (1792), these activists claimed that women were entitled to the same kind of "natural rights" as men. Men and women in essence — as rational and political beings — are the same, these feminists argued, so women ought to be given equal rights and equal opportunities.

Historically and philosophically, it can be useful to distinguish liberal feminism — with its more abstract concept of individual

21. Deborah Tannen, *You Just Don't Understand: Women and Men in Conversation* (New York: Ballantine, 1990), p. 15; her emphasis.
22. Sommers, p. 275.

human rights and its tendency to downplay the effects of gender — from gender feminism — which acknowledges and focuses on complementary differences between men and women. When her eighteenth-century society told the American Puritan Anne Bradstreet that her hand was better suited for a needle than "a poet's pen," she responded by seizing the disputed pen and writing philosophical heroic couplets that equaled many of those produced by the men of her time. That's liberal feminism at work. But Bradstreet also used her pen to write moving poems on being a wife and mother that ingeniously played with the idea that the pen can be employed as a kind of needle. For example, in "The Author to Her Book," she compares the book of her poems recently published in England without her knowledge to a poorly dressed child:

> Thou ill-formed offspring of my feeble brain,
> Who after birth didst by my side remain,
> Till snatched from thence by friends, less wise than true,
> Who thee abroad, exposed to public view,
> Made thee in rags, halting to th' press to trudge,
> Where errors were not lessened (all may judge).
> . . . .
> In better dress to trim thee was my mind,
> But nought save homespun cloth i' th' house I find.
>
> (ll. 1-6, 18-19)

Bradstreet thus insists that the metaphors and experiences of a woman's life, the "homespun cloth," have aesthetic value. That's gender feminism at work.

The practical reality is that many thinkers, like Bradstreet, find themselves somewhere in the middle of these dichotomies, sometimes drawing on the fact that woman are human beings, at other times drawing on the fact that women are women. Many feminists acknowledge that gender is *often* very important, but would not agree that gender is *always* the most important factor in every circumstance. Sometimes the needle; other times the pen. Jean Fox O'Barr, the director of the women's studies program at Duke, explains, "While feminist scholars do not maintain that every intellectual question and practical problem of interest has only gender dimensions, they argue that gender frequently informs other social dimensions."[23]

What is to prevent a women's studies program from teaching and debating these varying approaches, asking questions such as: What different kinds of feminism have evolved and what are their strengths and weaknesses? How has gender made a difference in history? How might it make a difference in the future? When might it not be significant? A good women's studies program, in my opinion, would expose students to the current diverse range of approaches to gender issues, including liberal feminism, gender feminism, and radical feminism.

What about some of the other alleged flaws in women's studies programs? Sommers claims that "the majority of women's studies classes are unscholarly, intolerant of dissent, and full of gimmicks."[24] If this is true, is it a result of poor teaching or an inherent problem in the field? Patai and Koertge claim it is a systemic problem since gender feminists repudiate science, logic, and critical thinking. However, only a few extremely radical feminists, such as Mary Daly, completely reject rationality. Most feminists ask the academy to consider the value of experience and intuition, in addition to the value of rationality and authority. And it is entirely possible to "question the assumptions and values of traditional scholarship"[25] without resorting to new-age, touchy-feely, logic-free mush.

In fact, the vast majority of work done in women's studies in the last thirty years consists of a great deal of so-called hard scholarship, compilations of new data (as in Carol Gilligan's case), archival work by historians and literary scholars (uncovering American women's role in the settling of the West, for example), a political philosophy that questions the dichotomy between "public" and "private" spheres of life. While there is certainly a lot of sloppy and unscholarly work produced in the field of women's studies, we can find equally unsound scholarship in other fields.

23. Jean Fox O'Barr, *Feminism in Action: Building Institutions & Community through Women's Studies* (Chapel Hill: University of North Carolina Press, 1994), p. 78.

24. Sommers, *Who Stole Feminism?* p. 90.

25. Patai and Koertge, *Professing Feminism,* p. 115.

Some of the original arguments advanced in favor of establishing women's studies programs were based on the discipline's intellectual rigor. Women's studies, Florence Howe argued in the late 1970s, is the perfect liberal art, accomplishing five objectives: (1) It is interdisciplinary and unifying; (2) it teaches skills in critical analysis; (3) it assumes a problem-solving stance; (4) it clarifies the issue of value judgment in education; and (5) it promotes socially useful ends.[26]

However, in Howe's last two objectives — clarifying value judgments and promoting socially useful ends — we find the site of much of the controversy. Sommers notes disparagingly that the goal of "equipping students to 'transform the world' is not quite the same as equipping them with the knowledge they need for getting on in the world." She cites disapprovingly the feminist philosopher Ann Ferguson's saying, "The goal of feminist teaching is not only to raise consciousness about . . . male domination system but also to create women and men who are agents of social change." These kinds of goals, says Sommers, inspire the gender feminists "with a missionary fervor unmatched by any other group in the contemporary academy."[27]

These transformational goals sit uneasily in what Mark Schwehn describes as today's Weberian-formed university, which extols the professor as the one who makes and transmits knowledge, rather than the one who forms character.[28] But attempting to create women and men who are agents of social change — isn't this very similar to Calvin College's own goal? Your mission statement includes the sentence, "Through our learning, we seek to be agents of renewal in the academy, church, and society." Similarly, my institution's goal, according to its catalog, is to develop scholar-servants with care and concern for other human beings and for creation. We are not institutions whose primary goal is "getting on in the world" in a profession, immersion in high culture, or the

26. Florence Howe, "Toward Women's Studies in the Eighties: Part 1," *Women's Studies Newsletter,* vol. 8, no. 4 (1979): 2.

27. Sommers, *Who Stole Feminism?* pp. 51-52.

28. Mark R. Schwehn, *Exiles from Eden: Religion and the Academic Vocation in America* (Oxford: Oxford University Press, 1993).

disinterested advancement of science. Rather, we believe, as Nick Wolterstorff puts it, "that the goal of Christian education is not just to *equip* students to live Christian lives but also to inspire and energize and dispose them to do so — that the goal is to contribute to their moral and spiritual *formation.*"[29]

Questioning values and assumptions is exactly the kind of task that we Christian scholars take on in our attempts to assess and reform culture, and we, too, at times move beyond rationality to draw upon "the substance of things hoped for, the evidence of things not seen" (Heb. 11:1). We acknowledge both special revelation and natural revelation, both religion and reason as sources for scholarly reflection. Our institutions are fundamentally constructed on the idea that "theoretical reason is not autonomous. Scholarly endeavors are not in general religiously neutral."[30] We understand that our values and beliefs inform what we do.

Committed teaching and scholarship are our hallmark. We cannot agree that goals to transform students and to rethink scholarship will doom an educational program. Certainly, the particular kind of transformation makes an important difference, as do the means of practicing that change, both of which must be worked out with fear and trembling. Our commitments and goals will obviously be different in some crucial ways from those of non-Christian institutions.

But the tension between presenting information and advocating a position is one with which the entire academic community has long struggled. This struggle has been exacerbated as the notion of a value-free, totally objective rationality has been deconstructed. These tensions recently were discussed at the Conference on the Role of Advocacy in the Classroom, sponsored by a number of academic professional organizations, including the Modern Language Association, the American Council of Learned Societies, and the American Association of University Professors. Most participants granted that advocacy — staking out and defending a position — is

---

29. Nicholas P. Wolterstorff, "Keeping Faith: Talks for New Faculty at Calvin College," *Occasional Papers from Calvin College*, vol. 7, no. 1 (February 1989): 56; his emphasis.

30. Ibid., p. 37.

inherent in academic life, but also agreed that using the classroom to proselytize or indoctrinate students is unacceptable. However, drawing the line between these two behaviors is often difficult. As Eric Hoffman, the executive director of the American Philosophical Association, stated, "Those who might in *theory* agree that advocacy is OK and indoctrination is not would often in practice apply the distinction in clashing ways."[31]

Teachers at Christian institutions struggle with some of the same issues, for we do not simply want to indoctrinate students into the Christian life. Neither do we always agree on issues such as of what the Christian mind might consist, or what kind of social or political transformation our society needs. But the secular academy faces a much greater obstacle when it comes to the question of forming character and creating agents of social change than we do, for the university, as many have noted, has become the multiversity, with little central mission, core, or coherence. Christian colleges, on the other hand, do have a central faith and mission. Sharing an overarching umbrella of values and beliefs, acknowledging that education includes both knowledge and transformation — Christian colleges are perfectly situated to develop unique, balanced, and strong women's studies programs. In so doing, we must ground these programs in our Christian beliefs and educational philosophy, particularly with respect to the role of women and gender in our world.

Gender studies in the Christian academy should be based on the principle that women and men are both equally valued by God. This foundational belief might be defined as *Christian feminism, evangelical feminism,* or *biblical feminism.* Mary Stewart Van Leeuwen describes the Christian feminist as "a person of either sex who sees women and men as *equally* saved, *equally* Spirit-filled and *equally* sent."[32] Rebecca Merrill Groothuis prefers the term *evangelical feminism.* Groothuis says that all models of feminism focus on "unjust and inequitable attitudes and behavior towards women," but that

31. Phyllis Franklin, "What Does Academic Freedom Really Mean?" *MLA Newsletter,* Fall 1995, p. 6.

32. Mary Stewart Van Leeuwen, *Gender and Grace: Love, Work & Parenting in a Changing World* (Downers Grove: InterVarsity Press, 1990), p. 36.

evangelical feminists draw upon the Bible as the final authority for describing this problem and diagnosing a solution.[33] Even Christian traditionalists who believe that women and men have specifically assigned roles in the home and church would be able to agree with either of these definitions, although they might differ in their practical applications of the principle.

Unlike liberal feminists, who depend solely upon the human rationality and autonomy proclaimed by the Enlightenment, Christian feminists also see human beings as creations of God, capable of rationality, but subject to sin and in need of salvation. Unlike radical feminists, Christian feminists see both kinds of sexism — patriarchy and matriarchy — as consequences of human sin. And unlike power feminists, Christian feminists are not working to liberate themselves or increase their own power, but to serve others. As Elaine Storkey writes, "A Christian feminist programme would [not] be the indulgent self-seeking which in many people's minds often epitomizes feminism today. . . . Following the tradition from which they come, Christian feminists will not be working and praying on their own account and from their own self-concerns, but to really help those to liberation who need it most."[34]

Women's studies at the Christian college should be guided by the comprehensive character of the Scriptures. For Calvinists, this will mean that women's studies will be pursued and related to the biblical narrative of creation, sin, and redemption. Reformed Christians understand that the sin of sexism leads to both personal and structural distortions of God's creation order. In *Gender and Grace*, Mary Stewart Van Leeuwen explains the gendered implications of the Genesis story in this way: As beings created in the image of God, men and women originally were mutually interdependent, both possessing an irreducibly social nature and both given dominion over creation. But the result of the fall, predicted by God in Genesis 3:16, is that men will have a tendency to let domination

---

33. Rebecca Merrill Groothuis, *Women Caught in the Conflict: The Culture War between Traditionalism and Feminism* (Grand Rapids: Baker, 1994), pp. 89, 109-10.

34. Elaine Storkey, *What's Right With Feminism?* (Grand Rapids: Eerdmans, 1985), p. 178.

replace dominion, while women's sociability will become social enmeshment, a debilitating tendency to preserve personal relationships no matter what the cost.[35] The Scriptures thus give us a basic understanding of gender inequities that, supported by the weight of evidence compiled during the past two decades of scholarship, provide the basis for a women's studies program.

Several schools in the Coalition of Christian Colleges and Universities (formerly the Christian College Coalition) have begun women's studies programs that attempt to build on a biblical worldview and the strength of the new gender studies scholarship while, at the same time, they try to avoid the lack of academic rigor and the surplus of radical politicization that characterize some programs. Although there may be more programs of which I am unaware, Wheaton College, Eastern College, Messiah College, and Seattle Pacific University all currently have minors that allow students the chance to think through gender issues with a Christian mind; to express, share, and critique feminist views in the light of biblical and theological traditions. Furthermore, the Oregon Extension of Houghton College has offered a successful Women Studies May Term for the past two years.

Gender studies at Christian colleges face their own set of obstacles, which tend to congregate more around the conservative backlash against feminism than the radical practice of identity politics. But as these programs take their first, wobbling baby-steps, we can take advantage of the fact that in some respects we stand outside the academic fray to study carefully and learn from the current breaches. We can learn at least four lessons from some of today's problems in women's studies programs.

First, following Gerald Graff's advice, women's studies programs in the Christian academy should be deliberately structured in such a way as to acknowledge and teach the conflicts in different views of feminism and gender. There are numerous ways to accomplish this goal — from the content of a particular course, to the curricular structure, to pedagogical practices. For example, the Introduction to Women's Studies that will be offered for the first time at Seattle Pacific this year includes an analysis and comparison of

35. Van Leeuwen, *Gender and Grace*, pp. 33-51.

liberal, Marxist, radical, and biblical feminism. Similarly, the Oregon Extension course called "Women in Literature and Psychology" includes this objective — "Students will gain an understanding of feminist thought and history" — which is achieved by reading and discussing the survey of the various feminisms presented in *After Eden,* the excellent volume produced by a Calvin Center for Christian Scholarship study team a few years ago.

While it is likely (although not mandatory) that most gender studies courses in the Christian academy will be taught by egalitarian biblical feminists, other views of gender and feminism held by Christians should also be presented, through readings, guest lectures, discussion, or debate. As in the academic presentation of any controversial issue, the opposing viewpoint should at least be described as honestly and fairly as possible. Gender studies in the Christian academy has the decided advantage of allowing a forum for all the voices concerned with women to have their say, including Christian feminists and traditionalists, who are all-too-frequently silenced in today's secular academy. The resulting discussions may also help to clarify some of the foundational and presuppositional differences between Christian feminists and those Christians with more traditionalist views.

As Mark Noll explains, those evangelicals "who hold that the Bible's central purpose is to communicate new life in the Spirit, or who feel that developments in modern western society are at least potentially instructive to Christians" differ in their attitudes toward feminism from "those who believe that the Bible in general teaches a divinely ordained chain of command, who hold that the Bible offers a detailed blueprint of God's will for everyday life, or who feel that western society has entered into an apocalyptic decline."[36] Most Reformed Christians would find themselves in the first camp, drawing upon both the Scriptures and the truths revealed through common grace in their interpretations. Differing approaches to women's issues in the Christian academy will thus also help highlight differing approaches to history, hermeneutics, and scholarship.

36. Mark A. Noll, *Between Faith and Criticism: Evangelicals, Scholarship, and the Bible in America,* 2nd ed. (Grand Rapids: Baker, 1991), p. 207.

Gender studies in the Christian academy will depart from the model provided by Graff in the fact that they will be based on an institutional mission that is much more specific than just teaching the conflicts. We do believe in, confess, and proclaim certain things. Programs in gender studies in the Christian academy should deliberately acknowledge that their assumptions and goals are formed by the general tenets of Christian feminism. Consequently, the advocacy — not indoctrination — that does take place in the gender studies classroom at the Christian college will have a clearly defined origin — which is not to say that all Christian feminists will agree on social policies, political positions, or aesthetic judgments. Nonetheless, students should be well aware that God's creation and equal love for women and men, God's endowment of talents on both men and women, and God's view of amicable human relations will inform what happens in the classroom and how the instructor approaches issues.

Third, gender studies programs must deliberately involve both men and women, as both professors and students. It is important that leadership come from both men and women. Wheaton provides a good model of this; their program originated through the efforts of Tom Kay, a historian, and Sarah Miles, a history and biology specialist. The official description of the Eastern minor states that it was "designed by faculty and administrators of both sexes and [is] intended for both men and women students." The Oregon Extension's May term faculty consists of two women and one man, and the student enrollment in this course has followed the national norm for women's studies courses, with 10 percent male and 90 percent female. In a recent course evaluation, all the participants agreed that male students should continue to be encouraged to enroll. Of course the challenge of all gender studies programs is to increase the number of male participants. At Eastern, an informational bulletin board on the minor was recently vandalized with the addition of the phrase, "Only non-male students need apply." An undaunted professor responded by substituting "mature" for "non," so that the graffiti read, "Only mature male students need apply."

Fourth, gender studies programs should maintain a distinctive, high-profile academic identity. Some of the biggest difficulties described by Patai and Koertge arose when the lines between the academic and the co-curricular women's programs became blurred. Consequently, instructors in some courses were not held to the same academic qualifications (advanced degree, etc.) as were other instructors, and staff members sometimes had too large a say in curricular matters. A co-curricular program focusing on gender issues is an essential aspect of a women's studies program, but women's studies also need to have a distinct academic identity. Wheaton has assured this identity by structural decisions such as having the minor fall under the jurisdiction of a specific faculty committee (the Interdisciplinary Studies Committee), by sponsoring a yearly academic conference, and by having academic co-chairs of the program who are available to the rest of the community for consulting on gender issues.

"One's goal as Christian scholar is not to be different but to be *faithful*" — I am quoting Nick Wolterstorff again, explaining Kuyper's way of seeing the relation of faith to learning.[37] Women's studies in the Christian academy must be faithful — to the revelation of the Scriptures, to the responsibility of the Christian scholar to act to reform the world, to recent intellectual discoveries and academic progress. In so doing, we can fruitfully embrace some of the most significant tensions in our time, those between men and women.

37. Wolterstorff, "Keeping Faith," p. 37; his emphasis.

The Supreme Court, Societal Elites, and Calvin College: Christian Higher Education in a Secular Age

Stephen V. Monsma

In 1987 Phillip Bishop was an assistant professor in physiology and physical education at the University of Alabama.[1] In one of his classes he explained to his students that he was a Christian believer, and that that "bias" — as he termed it — affected his approach to his academic duties. He also invited students to an after-class, purely voluntary session where he lectured and led a discussion on evidences for God in human physiology. Professor Bishop's departmental chair sent him a memo in which he stated that Bishop must refrain from such activities. The university administration supported the department chair, and a legal battle ensued. The United States District Court ruled in favor of Professor Bishop being able to make such minimal references to his Christian faith, but the United States Court of Appeals overturned the District Court and upheld the university's action. The American Association of University Professors — which normally leaps to the defense of professors whose academic freedom has been violated to the slightest degree — declined to get involved. The United States Supreme Court refused to hear the case. Professor Bishop was effectively muzzled.

One could view this incident as a rare example of hostility

---

1. The following information on this incident is taken from the decision of the U.S. Court of Appeals. See *Bishop v. Aronov* (926 F.2d 1066) 1991. Also see the account of it in Phillip E. Johnson, *Reason in the Balance* (Downers Grove: InterVarsity Press, 1995), pp. 173-78.

toward religion. But such an interpretation would be wrong: it is neither rare nor, do I believe, rooted in hostility toward religion. I strongly suspect that the University of Alabama's position was animated by a worldview that places religion, and Christianity in particular, outside the proper scope of academia. The appeals court decision reflected such a perspective when it stated: "The University has not suggested that Dr. Bishop cannot hold his particular [religious] views . . . ; nor could it so prohibit him. The University has simply said that he may not discuss his religious beliefs or opinions under the guise of University courses."[2] In the court's view, it was not being anti-religious. It was only saying that religious beliefs simply have no place in a university classroom; to bring them in is to slip something in that does not belong in a genuine academic course.

Neither is this incident a rare example of religion being seen as illegitimate when brought into academia. In 1988 a subcommittee of the American Association of University Professors echoed the reasoning of the appeals court when it argued that religiously based colleges and universities forfeit their "moral right to proclaim themselves as authentic seats of higher learning" and are not institutions in the same class as those without religious commitments.[3] That great icon of our materialistic age, *Money* magazine, refuses to list religiously based colleges and universities in its annual "Best College Buys." It proclaims without apparent embarrassment that it does not list "colleges where religious study of any nature . . . is a significant academic requirement."[4] Phi Beta Kappa has rejected applications for chapters at Mormon Brigham Young University and most Catholic colleges and universities due to their religious standards.[5]

These are all examples of the prevailing view of religion's illegitimacy in the American academy. Whether it is a matter of

2. *Bishop v. Aronov,* at 1076.
3. See Michael W. McConnell, "Academic Freedom in Religious Colleges and Universities," *Law and Contemporary Problems* 53 (1990): 309.
4. "How We Rank the Colleges," *Money Guide: Best College Buys* (1996 ed.), p. 23.
5. On Brigham Young University see "Honor Society Rejects Membership Bid," *Chronicle of Higher Education,* 3 June 1992, p. A4; on the Catholic colleges see George M. Marsden, *The Soul of the American University* (New York: Oxford University Press, 1994), pp. 437-38.

Christian perspectives and insights in secular colleges and universities or Christian colleges and universities within the world of American higher education, religion is often viewed as a purely private matter with no legitimate role in academia. When someone seeks to bring religion into academe, it is seen as an embarrassment — somewhat like the black sheep of the family that shows up at a family wedding in cut-off jeans and more than slightly inebriated.

Viewing religion in academia as illegitimate is a recent development. At the beginning of the twentieth century American higher education was marked by a host of deeply religious private colleges and universities within the Protestant and Catholic traditions of Christianity and even state colleges and universities were marked by clearly religious atmospheres. In this essay I do not, however, seek to retell the story of the delegitimation of religion in the American academy. Historian George Marsden and others have already ably done so.[6] What I seek to do instead is, first, to explore how certain key Supreme Court decisions and the reasoning underlying them both reflect and reinforce the beliefs of societal elites that have contributed to the delegitimation of religion in academia. Next, I will suggest some recent, still evolving, yet hopeful signs from the Supreme Court that may eventually help support a relegitimation of religion in higher education. Third, I suggest the role Calvin College and Christian scholars in other colleges and universities need to play in relegitimating the role of Christianity in higher education.

The Supreme Court and Religion in Academia

The Supreme Court is a law-making body whose legal interpretations are binding on all of society. But this obvious fact ought not to blind one to the equally accurate and significant observation that it is also both a mirror reflecting the beliefs and values of the American people — and especially the beliefs and values of the

6. See Marsden, *Soul of the University,* and George M. Marsden and Bradley J. Longfield, eds., *The Secularization of the Academy* (New York: Oxford University Press, 1992).

highly educated, culturally dominant elites in society — and an independent force making its own contribution to the beliefs and values of the American people. Thus the decisions of the Supreme Court as they relate to church and state are revealing of the perspectives and assumptions with which dominant American elites view religion and its relationship to the world of higher education; these decisions also add to and reinforce those perspectives and assumptions.

In the post–World War II era the Supreme Court made a series of decisions that held that all government aid to religion was contrary to the establishment clause of the First Amendment, largely in the context of several states' attempts to extend financial assistance to nonpublic elementary and secondary schools. In the 1947 landmark case of *Everson v. Board of Education* the Court declared in ringing words:

> No tax in any amount, large or small, can be levied to support any religious activities or institutions, whatever they may be called, or whatever form they may adopt to teach or practice religion. Neither a state nor the Federal government can, openly or secretly, participate in the affairs of any religious organizations or groups and *vice versa*. In the words of Jefferson, the clause against establishment of religion by law was intended to erect "a wall of separation between church and state."[7]

Later it went on to insist that the wall between church and state "must be kept high and impregnable."[8] In short, there was to be an impenetrable wall between church and state that would prevent the government from participating in the affairs of religion and religion from participating in the affairs of government. The Supreme Court thereby established as a bedrock constitutional principle that no aid may go to religion.

The implicit assumption in this position is that a wall of separation of this nature does not harm and even protects both religion and government. Religion will still be fully free to be all

7. *Everson v. Board of Education,* 330 U.S. at 16 (1947).
8. Ibid., at 18.

that it should be and government to be all that it should be. But this is only true if one accepts a perspective on religion and society rooted in Enlightenment thinking, a perspective that ever since the founding era and figures such as Thomas Jefferson and James Madison has had a profound influence in the United States. Both Jefferson and Madison saw religion — outside of consensual beliefs rooted in common sense — as being divisive, not subject to reason, and a private matter that was unimportant for the public life of the nation. Historian Thomas Buckley once wrote that Thomas Jefferson "considered theological statements . . . to be simply 'opinion,' based not on reason, but on revelations unacceptable to a thoughtful man." He then went on to write, "In the Jeffersonian scheme of things, the religious dimension of personal belief was private, absolutely. He repeated it in a multitude of ways."[9] The well-known Catholic scholar John Courtney Murray once summarized James Madison's perspective when he wrote: "For Madison, as for John Locke, . . . religion is of its nature a personal, private, interior matter of the individual conscience, having no relevance to the public concerns of the state."[10]

What the Supreme Court did in 1947 was to read into the First Amendment Jefferson's and Madison's Enlightenment view of religion as a purely private matter with no legitimate role in the public realm. In so doing, it had the support of most of society's elites. *The Washington Post,* for example, editorialized at the time, "The religious function is wholly private."[11] Similarly, former Speaker of the House of Representatives, Tom Foley, once said: "Let me point out that I'm a Roman Catholic, and I've never — never — allowed my religion to affect my position on public policy."[12] How can this

---

9. Thomas E. Buckley, "The Political Theology of Thomas Jefferson," in Merrill D. Peterson and Robert C. Vaughan, eds., *The Virginia Statute for Religious Freedom* (Cambridge: Cambridge University Press, 1988), p. 90.

10. John Courtney Murray, "Law or Prepossessions?" *Law and Contemporary Problems* 14 (1949): 29.

11. "Church and State," *The Washington Post,* 13 February 1947. Reprinted in Terry Eastland, ed., *Religious Liberty in the Supreme Court* (Washington, D.C.: Ethics and Public Policy Center, 1993), p. 81.

12. Quoted in Nancy Traver, "Breakfast with the Speaker," *Time Bureau Chiefs' Report* (*Time* Magazine Company, 1992), p. 2.

be? The Catholic tradition is rich in a host of insights highly relevant to public policy, insights ably articulated by Catholic academics, the United States Catholic Conference, and many Catholic periodicals. The problem is that the tradition of Catholic political and social thought is at war with the Enlightenment-rooted tradition that seeks to privatize religion. In Foley's case, Enlightenment thinking has won out. He apparently sees his Catholic faith as a personal, private matter without relevance to the political and social realms.

The Enlightenment-rooted position of Jefferson, Madison, and most societal elites today, however, is not and never has been universally accepted. Most deeply religious persons — and certainly most Christians — see their religious beliefs as having profound implications for the public life of society. Assuming that religion has only a truncated, privatized role in society, as the Supreme Court has done, does violence to the nature of religion. In the words of John Courtney Murray, the Supreme Court adopted "an irredeemable piece of sectarian dogmatism."[13] As Murray pointed out, the paradox could not be greater: In the name of no-establishment of religion the Supreme Court established a sectarian secular creed.

In spite of the no-aid-to-religion, wall of separation rhetoric used by the Supreme Court, it has over the years permitted a variety of governmental actions that accommodate or assist religion. There is some irony in the fact that the same early decision that insisted there be a "high and impregnable" wall between church and state and that no tax money could go to support religion, actually approved the program of aid to religious schools that was under challenge — a New Jersey program that paid for the bus transportation of children to religious schools. The Supreme Court has also approved a crèche as part of a public Christmas display, prayers at the start of legislative sessions, and aid to religious hospitals, counseling centers, and colleges. One could be tempted to conclude that perhaps the Supreme Court has been more supportive of a public role for religion and thus has not contributed to the delegitimation of religion in academia as much as its 1947 *Everson* decision would indicate.

13. Murray, "Law or Prepossessions?" p. 30.

Unfortunately, a careful reading of these decisions does not support this conclusion. The Supreme Court sought to maintain its no-aid-to-religion position, while at the same time approving programs that recognized or aided religious practices or organizations, largely on three bases, all of which reaffirmed a purely private role for religion. One is the notion that in certain contexts what appears to be religious has in fact been largely secularized. Justice William Brennan once articulated this concept in embarrassingly clear terms:

> I would suggest that such practices as the designation of "In God We Trust" as our national motto, or the references to God contained in the Pledge of Allegiance to the flag can best be understood . . . as a form of "ceremonial deism," protected from Establishment Clause scrutiny chiefly because they have lost through rote repetition any significant religious content. . . . Their message is dominantly secular.[14]

It is on this basis that prayers at the start of legislative sessions, a crèche in Pawtucket, Rhode Island, and a menorah in the Pittsburgh city hall were found constitutional.

A second basis on which the Supreme Court has at times allowed public funds in support of religious organizations was largely developed in the context of public funds and religiously based colleges and universities. It is the sacred-secular distinction. The aid programs under challenge could be approved because the Supreme Court was willing to accept the separability of the secular and sacred aspects of education at religiously based colleges. Therefore, it could accept the theory that public funds were supporting the secular aspects, but not the religious aspects of the colleges. By making a clear-cut distinction between the religious and secular elements in a college education and then only funding the secular elements, one can have government financial aid to a religious college without aiding religion (at least in legal theory). In one of its decisions the Supreme Court noted that "the secular and sectarian activities of the colleges were easily separated" and that "the colleges perform

14. *Lynch v. Donnelly,* 465 U.S. at 716-17 (1984).

'essentially secular educational functions' that are distinct and separable from religious activity."[15]

The Supreme Court thereby approved aid to religious colleges and universities, but on the basis of reasoning fully in keeping with the Enlightenment concept of religion as private belief. Religion was viewed as a separate, segregated aspect of higher education, and aid was to go only to colleges' nonreligious aspects.

This reasoning can be more clearly seen in the third basis on which the Supreme Court has sometimes held governmental support of religious organizations to be constitutional. It has ruled that religiously based organizations are eligible for public funds only if they are not "pervasively sectarian." In one case Justice Lewis Powell, speaking for a 6-3 majority, wrote: "Aid normally may be thought to have a primary effect of advancing religion when it flows to an institution in which religion is so pervasive that a substantial portion of its functions are subsumed in the religious mission. . . ."[16] He then went on to make the point that the college whose receiving of government funds was under challenge was not marked by a pervasively religious nature such as this and thus could receive those funds.

In other words, religious colleges' and universities' ability to receive public funds was made dependent on their not being so thoroughly religious that their secular aspects could not be split off from their religious aspects. Thus, the Court thereby maintained the principle that colleges' religious aspects were ineligible for public support.

In all these cases, one finds the Supreme Court reflecting the same position as that present in the examples cited at the beginning of this essay, namely, that introducing religion into higher education is illegitimate and destructive of "real" education. Whenever the Supreme Court says a "high and impregnable wall" must separate the worlds of public affairs and of religion, and whenever it says government may only recognize and honor religion when it is no longer taken very seriously, whenever it says government may aid religious

15. *Roemer v. Maryland Public Works Board,* 426 U.S. at 762 and 764 (1976). The quoted words are from the lower court's decision.
16. *Hunt v. McNair,* 413 U.S. at 743 (1973).

colleges only when they are not thoroughly religious and when their religious aspects have been segregated out from their secular aspects and then only the secular aspects aided, the legitimacy of religion as a vibrant force in society in any serious sense is drawn into question.

It is hard to draw a direct cause-and-effect line between the Supreme Court's no-aid-to-religion decisions and the delegitimation of religion in American higher education noted earlier, but the parallels between the beliefs and assumptions of the Supreme Court and other societal elites are striking. The message — and the underlying worldview — is the same: Religion is a personal, private matter whose legitimate role in the public life of the nation, including higher education, is at best very limited. The University of Alabama, *Money* magazine, Phi Beta Kappa, the American Association of University Professors, *The Washington Post,* and the Supreme Court are all operating out of the same mind-set or worldview. The Supreme Court has not been the answer to societal trends delegitimating religion in higher education; it has been part of the problem.

The Equal Treatment Strain in Supreme Court Reasoning

There is, fortunately, a second, more hopeful strain in the Supreme Court's First Amendment interpretations and legal reasoning that also needs to be considered. Since the 1980s it has run parallel to the no-aid-to-religion line of reasoning, and in two key 1995 decisions it received new, dramatic development by the Court. Just as the old wall of separation, no-aid-to-religion line of reasoning both reflected and contributed to the beliefs that resulted in the delegitimation of religion in higher education, this new line of reasoning holds the potential for playing a role in the relegitimation of religion in higher education.

This new line of reasoning is the equal treatment or equal access strain. It is currently evolving, and whether it one day will replace the no-aid-to-religion strain, will partially replace it, or will simply peter out and be forgotten is unknown. It thus far has had only limited application. Nonetheless the equal treatment line of reasoning is relevant to the role of religion in higher education.

This strain of jurisprudence was first clearly articulated in *Wid-*

mar v. Vincent, a 1981 case that ruled against a policy of the University of Missouri at Kansas City that excluded religious student groups from using university facilities for their meetings. Justice Lewis Powell, in the Court's majority opinion, argued that excluding religious student groups from the use of university facilities available to all other groups violated their right to free speech and association. Then he went on to conclude that allowing the religious group to use public facilities would not violate the Establishment Clause of the First Amendment. He wrote that "an 'equal access' policy would [not] be incompatible with this Court's Establishment Clause cases."[17] Later he poured more content into the concept of "equal access" when he noted that the university had created an open forum "that is available to a broad class of nonreligious as well as religious speakers" and that "an open forum in a public university does not confer any imprimatur of state approval on religious sects or practices."[18]

The importance of both the availability of a public forum or benefit to a wide variety of religious and nonreligious groups and the absence of any actual or implied governmental endorsement or approval of religious groups and beliefs were to prove crucial in the Court's subsequent development of the equal treatment line of reasoning. Three cases are especially helpful in seeing its development.[19]

A 1993 decision dealt with a school district's turning down the request of a church to rent its auditorium to show a series of religiously based films on child rearing. The Supreme Court's unanimous opinion held that since the school district's "property had repeatedly been used by a wide variety of private organizations,"[20] refusing to rent to a religious group violated that group's free speech rights. In addition, the Court held that renting a public school facility to a religious group would not violate the Establishment Clause, since "as in *Widmar,* there would have been no realistic danger that the community would think that the district was en-

17. *Widmar v. Vincent,* 454 U.S. at 271 (1981).
18. Ibid., at 275.
19. In addition to the cases discussed in this section, the equal access strain also played a major role in *Witters v. Washington Department of Services for the Blind,* 474 U.S. 481 (1988), *Westside Community Schools v. Mergens,* 58 LW 4720 (1990), and *Zobrest v. Catalina Foothills School District,* 125 L Ed 2d 1 (1993).
20. *Lamb's Chapel v. Center Moriches School District,* 1993 LW 187864, at 5.

dorsing religion or any particular creed. . . ."[21] The concepts of nonendorsement of religion and government's equal treatment of religious and nonreligious groups were more important in the Court's thinking than a strict no-aid-to-religion standard and whatever benefits were being given religion.

In 1995 the Supreme Court handed down two decisions that significantly strengthened the equal treatment line of reasoning. One dealt with the placing of a cross on the grounds of the Ohio state capitol. In this case the Court held that there was no Establishment Clause violation by Ohio's permitting the display of the cross. Justice Scalia, writing for a plurality of the Court, relied on equal treatment reasoning:

> The State did not sponsor respondents' expression, the expression was made on government property that had been opened to the public for speech, and permission was requested . . . on the same terms required of other private groups. . . . We find it peculiar to say that government "promotes" or "favors" a religious display by giving it the same access to a public forum that all other displays enjoy. . . . [I]t is no violation for government to enact neutral policies that happen to benefit religion.[22]

There was no attempt to talk of the cross as having been secularized in the context of the display at issue, as there had been earlier with other religious displays in public places. Equal treatment, without watering down the religious nature of the symbol at issue, was the key.

A second key 1995 equal treatment decision is *Rosenberger v. Rector.* The University of Virginia had refused to fund a Christian student publication, even though it had funded fifteen other student opinion publications. In a close 5-4 vote the Supreme Court held that the university's refusal to fund the publication violated the students' free speech rights, and that funding it would not violate the Establishment Clause. In his majority opinion, Justice Anthony Kennedy used the language of neutrality more than the

21. Ibid., at 5-6.
22. *Capitol Square Review Board v. Pinette,* 1995 WL 38063, at 6.

language of equal treatment, yet the opinion is clearly rooted in the equal treatment line of reasoning. He wrote:

> A central lesson of our decisions is that a significant factor in upholding governmental programs in the face of Establishment Clause attack is their neutrality towards religion. . . . We have held that the guarantee of neutrality is respected, not offended, when the government, following neutral criteria and evenhanded policies, extends benefits to recipients whose ideologies and viewpoints, including religious ones, are broad and diverse.[23]

A program funding a religious publication was saved from First Amendment violation since religion was not singled out for favored treatment and the funding was extended to "the whole spectrum of speech, whether it manifests a religious view, an antireligious view, or neither."[24]

The reasoning in this case is in sharp contrast to that used in the earlier, no-aid-to-religion cases. That fact was not lost on the four dissenting justices. They clearly saw that the no-aid-to-religion principle and the sacred-secular distinction under which religious institutions have sometimes been permitted to receive public funds were being undermined by the *Rosenberger* decision. They wrote:

> Even when the Court [in the past] has upheld aid to an institution performing both secular and sectarian functions, it has always made a searching enquiry to ensure that the institution kept the secular activities separate from its sectarian ones, with any direct aid flowing only to the former and never the latter.[25]

They went on to advocate the continued reliance on "the no-direct-funding principle" over "the principle of evenhandedness" of funding.[26]

In summary, there is a recent, developing strain within the Supreme Court's jurisprudence that runs parallel to and is in tension

23. *Rosenberger v. Rector*, 1995 WL 382046, at 10-11.
24. Ibid., at 11.
25. Ibid., at 24.
26. Ibid., at 27.

with the no-aid-to-religion line of reasoning. It allows limited forms of governmental accommodation and assistance to religiously based groups and activities, as long as that accommodation and assistance is offered equally to all religious groups and activities and to religious and nonreligious groups and activities on the same basis. Equal treatment is the key to passing constitutional muster; not a separability of religious and secular aspects of a religious organization, with the religious relegated to the purely private realm. When religious groups and activities may not be excluded from public recognition or support that parallel, nonreligious groups and activities are receiving — even without giving up or segregating their deeply religious aspects — clearly the no-aid-to-religion principle and the sacred-secular and pervasively sectarian distinctions are being ignored, if not overthrown. Whether this new, equal treatment line of reasoning on the Supreme Court will ever become the settled law of the land is uncertain. Two strains of reasoning are today vying for dominance. One or the other may win out in the future, or an accommodation between the two may be found.

The equal treatment line of reasoning carries with it a potential to play a role in relegitimating religion in American higher education because at its heart lies the concept of allowing religion to be what it is with whatever strength or weakness, appeal or disfavor inheres in it. This is in sharp contrast to the mind-set in which the no-aid-to-religion, wall of separation approach is rooted. That approach says religion should be kept walled off from "secular" society in its various aspects and manifestations; equal treatment says religion is to be accepted on equal terms with secular belief systems or movements of a similar or parallel nature. Religion is to be accepted as a legitimate, appropriate aspect of public society. It is to be accorded no special position or special favor; neither is it to be placed under any special liability or disadvantage. Government is to be neutral toward practices and organizations of all religious faiths and of none. But that neutrality often can only be achieved by government granting religion the same recognition and advantages as those given nonreligious organizations and belief structures.

Admittedly, in the three decisions just reviewed — and in other, similar decisions — the Supreme Court did not deal directly with the legitimacy of religion in higher education. Nor did it deal with the actions of college accrediting agencies, university hiring committees, the American Association of University Professors, and the news media — all of whom will have to change if the relegitimation of religion in academia is to be achieved. Nevertheless, just as the Supreme Court both reflected and reinforced broader societal forces in its adoption of the no-aid-to-religion, wall of separation approach to religion in the public square, so also the new equal treatment approach — if fully adopted and broadly applied — has a great potential to have an impact on societal beliefs that go much beyond that approach's specific legal impact.

Calvin College and the Relegitimation of Religion in Higher Education

The equal treatment line of reasoning constitutes an opportunity that may lead to religion in general and Christianity in particular being once again accepted as having something of worth to contribute to the academic enterprise. Whether or not what is now only an opportunity or an opening actually leads to such a result depends, in part, on the Supreme Court, the academy, and other societal elites and their reactions to this new line of reasoning. But it depends as much or more on the reactions of the community of Christian scholars and institutions.

The defects in the Supreme Court's wall of separation, no-aid-to-religion doctrine and its contribution to the delegitimation of religion in academia are clear. Many who agree with this conclusion routinely blame the Supreme Court and secular church-state separationist groups such as the American Civil Liberties Union for this situation. I believe, however, that much of the blame must rest with the Christian community. I have argued elsewhere that throughout the nineteenth century, when theologically conservative Protestants were the culturally dominant force in the United States, almost no thought was given to developing a theoretically sound approach to church-state relations.[27] Old church-state separation concepts

27. See Stephen V. Monsma, *Positive Neutrality: Letting Religious Freedom Ring* (Westport, Conn.: Greenwood, 1993), esp. chap. 3.

rooted more in the Enlightenment concepts of Jefferson and Madison than in Christian thinking tended to dominate, even when practice was quite different. When in the twentieth century the gales of increasing religious pluralism and secularism struck, there was no firm basis on which to defend an appropriate role for religion in the public life of the nation.

When one reads the Supreme Court opinions from the thirty years following World War II one is struck by the theoretically more sophisticated arguments that were often made by those attacking the government's accommodating or supporting religion than by those supporting it. I do not blame justices such as Stanley Reed, Potter Stewart, and Byron White, who fought to stem the tide with weak concepts and inadequate theories. I do blame the broader Christian community that thought so little about basic issues that justices sympathetic to religion playing a legitimate role in public life were left without the concepts and theories they needed to make their case.

Even today many — including many Christians — have no ready answer to the question of what Christianity and other religions have to offer biology, history, literature, political science, and a host of other disciplines. The model too many persons have in mind when one mentions religion in academe is heavy-handed proselytizing, attempts to substitute a seven-day creation account for the gradual development of the creation, and an extreme right-wing political agenda.

The Christian community — including the Catholic, Mormon, and evangelical Protestant communities — as well as the communities of religious traditions such as Orthodox Judaism and Islam may be about to be given a second chance. That is what I see in the equal treatment line of reasoning. It is an opportunity, an opening, but if it is actually to result in a relegitimation of religion in academe — as well as elsewhere in the public life of the nation — the Christian community must take the lead in developing theories, principles, and concepts justifying and articulating the legitimate role of religion in academe. Others are not going to do it for us.

In what follows I do not want to strike a triumphalistic note, as though Christian scholars and institutions can force the relegitimation of religion in academia by their own efforts. Success or failure in such attempts is ultimately God's doing, not ours.

Nevertheless, God calls Christian scholars to be faithful, and in this context I am convinced that faithful Christian scholarship means developing a clear, theoretically sophisticated case for why Christianity and other religious traditions should have access to academia on a par with other worldviews and systems of thought — why they deserve equal treatment — and then articulating that case in a persuasive, winsome manner. Based on the old saw that a picture is worth a thousand words, a large part of articulating the role of religion in academia consists of Christian academics creating compelling models of Christian scholarship.

Let no one underestimate the task that I have just described. Original, creative Christian scholarship is difficult, and the world-views that argue that such scholarship is impossible or illegitimate are deeply entrenched in our culture. It will take persistent, organized, coordinated efforts, and the commitment of major resources, to accomplish it. Yet without it, I am convinced that the equal treatment line of reasoning now observable on the Supreme Court, with all of its potential in both the political and academic worlds, will either wither and die or remain limited and truncated in its application.

The sort of effort for which I am calling will take the combined efforts of many persons and institutions. Individual scholars laboring in secular institutions have a role to play, as is true of scholars in Mormon institutions such as Brigham Young University, in Catholic institutions such as the University of Notre Dame and Catholic University, and in Jewish institutions such as Yeshiva University. But I think I am engaging in more than personal sentimentalism when I say that Calvin College may have a special role to play. I make this bold a claim essentially for two reasons. One is that Calvin is the leading North American institutionalized expression of the Reformed, Kuyperian perspective on learning. Some of those at Dordt College, Trinity College, the Institute for Christian Studies, and elsewhere may dispute this claim! But in terms of length of existence, size, reputation, strength of faculty, financial stability, and numbers of graduates and former faculty in positions of influence in American society, I believe this case can be made without in any way ignoring or downplaying the considerable contributions being made by other centers of Reformed learning.

Adding to the strategic position Calvin College occupies is my belief that the Reformed, Kuyperian school of thought forms the foundation for the most compelling case for the equal treatment of religion in academia. At the heart of the Reformed perspective on learning is the famous statement of Abraham Kuyper, "There is not one square inch of the entire creation about which Jesus Christ does not cry out, 'This is mine! This belongs to me!'"[28] Our God reigns over all of creation. And because he reigns, his word and his will are relevant to all of creation. There is no neutral science, no neutral learning. This perspective is the essential answer that needs to be given to the Supreme Court and societal elites when they see religion as relevant only to one's personal life and an irrelevant distraction in the public realm.

A second reason I see Calvin as having an essential role to play in the relegitimation of religion in academia is its strategic position in the religious landscape of North America. The very tensions in Calvin's tradition being celebrated in these inaugural ceremonies enable Calvin to speak to and be heard by various streams within American Christianity. It is close enough to the evangelical tradition of American Protestantism that it can speak to and be respectfully listened to by that tradition. It is well known and respected within the Coalition for Christian Colleges and Universities. In short, Calvin has the potential to have an influence on the broader evangelical world. Yet it is also in a stronger position to speak to and be heard by the Roman Catholic tradition than is the rest of evangelicalism. With its developing ties to the University of Notre Dame, its tradition of strong scholarship, and its absence of a fundamentalist past, Calvin College has a basis on which to engage in dialogue with and build solidarity with the Catholic community.

But for Calvin College to live up to its full potential and fulfill the task being set before it, Calvin will also need to change. It needs to rise to even higher plateaus of scholarship and of creative efforts to reach beyond its Christian Reformed heritage and to speak effectively to American culture. It therefore needs to take such steps as creating more endowed chairs, which will give first-rate scholars

28. Quoted in Richard J. Mouw, *Uncommon Decency* (Downers Grove: InterVarsity Press, 1992), p. 147.

the time and resources needed to develop and articulate their thinking. It needs to strengthen the Calvin Center for Christian Scholarship, the Social Research Center, and the Meeter Center for Calvin Studies, and perhaps establish other centers or institutes that will bring together a broad range of Christian scholars for reflection, mutual stimulation, and joint writing ventures. And I personally am convinced that Calvin needs to move in the direction of graduate education, as soon as the time is ripe.

Steps such as these will help Calvin College to achieve its full promise and potential. The nature and meaning of Christian scholarship would thereby be further developed, defended, and modeled. As this happens, the equal treatment line of reasoning emerging on the Supreme Court may — by God's grace — grow into a foundation on which the legitimate role of Christianity and other religions in American higher education will again be affirmed and accepted.

"Dutch" and Reformed and "Black" and Reformed in South Africa: A Tale of Two Traditions on the Move to Unity and Responsibility

Russel Botman

"Today, all of us do, by our presence here . . . confer glory and hope. . . . Out of the experience of an extraordinary human disaster that lasted too long, must be born a society of which all humanity will be proud."[1]

These were the words of President Nelson Mandela on that beautiful day of 10 May 1994 when he was inaugurated as the first democratically elected president of South Africa. He was speaking like an expectant father. Having spoken of the birth of a new society, the president continued to explain to the people that the delivery will require midwives and men. As if this was not frightening enough, he said that the total South African community will have to shoulder this responsibility.

"Fat chance, Mister President," was my first reaction. "Which South Africa are you talking about?" And then I was reminded that

1. Nelson Mandela, *Long Walk to Freedom* (Raudburg, South Africa: Macdonald Purnell, 1994), p. 613.

85

President Mandela actually attended the first General Synod of the Uniting Reformed Church in Southern Africa in April 1994. So I said to myself, "I understand, you want this synod that unites the two black Reformed churches, as representatives of the victims of apartheid, to act as the 'wounded healers of South Africa.'" I thought: "This is theologically sound, drawing on the best traditions in practical theology!" But then President Mandela decided to really challenge the black Reformers by also attending the General Synod of the "Dutch" Reformed Church in October 1994. In his address to the synod he called on them as well to participate in the birth of a "society of which all humanity will be proud!" Then I realized that he was actually challenging the most divided religious community in South Africa both to overcome their historical differences and to participate in unison in the building of a new South African nation. By visiting these two synods he indicated that the country expects a significant contribution to nation building from all Reformed people in South Africa.

The well-known Reformed South African theologian, pastor, and prophet Beyers Naudé, one of the few who earned the right to speak on the behalf of the Dutch Reformers as well as the black Reformers, had said, already in the late eighties, that "something new is groaning to emerge which will *(would)* challenge the whole church in South Africa to the depths of its being."[2] Since this statement was made a number of articles and books appeared asking what kind of challenge the historical breath of fresh air brings to theology and the calling of the church. Issues of theological renewal started to fill the air, yearning for and surging toward "the new thing that God was doing among us."

Dirkie Smit, the highly regarded systematic theologian at the University of the Western Cape, summarized his description of the tensions in Reformed theology in South Africa by saying that "Reformed theology in South Africa is undergoing radical and dramatic changes. It will not survive in its present state. It has been too integrated into a South African society that is being transformed to remain unaffected."[3] And I think he is right. However, many Re-

2. Quoted in Albert Nolan, *God in South Africa: The Challenge of the Gospel* (Cape Town: Philips, 1988), p. 5.
3. D. J. Smit, "Reformed Theology in South Africa," *Acta Theologica* 1 (1992): 88-110.

formed people, on first sight, will find it hard to understand these words. And Smit correctly argued that the reason for this has to do with the plurality in Reformed theology. He continued: "South Africa's story has, for many years, been the well-known *tale of two cities*, or more precisely, the tale of many cities. South Africans live in worlds apart. . . . Our common faith, tradition and confessional heritage were not strong enough to break the historical barriers of ethnicity, class and racism."[4]

I would like to open a window on only two of the many Reformed discourses, that is, the discourse between Dutch Reformers and black Reformers. Unlike Dutch Calvinism in North America, which, according to James Bratt, stayed "ethnic" and "evangelical" but remained a "subculture," ethnic and evangelical Dutch Calvinism in South Africa became the dominant culture. In the new South Africa the discourse between Dutch Reformers and black Reformers has become a major challenge to theology. The fact that the Dutch Reformed Mission Church and the Dutch Reformed Church in Africa have united in 1994 to form the Uniting Reformed Church represents a major partner in dialogue with the Dutch Reformers who are members of the white Dutch Reformed Church. These two communities now meet to discuss issues of church unity, reconciliation, and justice. As one of those directly involved in this process, I would like to share the story of these two communities as they struggle to overcome the great divide of apartheid and its Calvinistic theological justification.

The most central quest in Calvinism lies in coming to terms with the calling of God within the concrete context. For Calvinists this quest is by nature a biblical and contextual search for meaning and responsibility. It receives a profound significance when the overriding context is one of nation building. South Africa now stands at the very dawn of a process of nation building, as evidenced by the theme of President Mandela's presidential inauguration on 10 May 1994, namely, *Many Cultures, One Nation*. The politics and the theology of nation building are at the heart of the South African agenda. Keeping the faith in South Africa in the context of the discourse between Dutch Reformers and black Reformers means

4. Ibid.

coming to terms with the task of nation building in a divided house. To appreciate this, one has to understand that South Africa is still suffering from its former nation-building project, which was also primarily engineered by Dutch Reformers.

J. D. du Toit (Totius), addressing the People's Congress of 1944, said, "The emergence of nations and kingdoms is approved by Scripture." He argued that the God of the Bible is revealed in the creation story as *Hammabdil*, the great Divider or Division-maker. Every single day of creation was a day of God creating division. It is not enough to know and believe that God created day and night or male and female. It is more important to know and believe that God separated them from each other. The entire story of creation is centrally about God setting things and creatures apart from one another. To his mind it was indeed possible to ask a divided society to give birth to a nation. It is precisely for this purpose, he said, that God has given them the specific command to fill the earth (Gen. 1 and 9), which means moving away from one another. This, he told his audience, constitutes the central quest of nation building. The story of the tower of Babel reaffirmed segregation as a theology of nation building. Nations are biblically called to set themselves up against the Babylonian spirit of "the melting pot" theory, which destroys the dividing work of God. At this juncture of his speech he referred (and with more than great admiration) to Abraham Kuyper's support for the Deadly Afrikaner Trek from the Cape into the interior of South Africa. He reminded his audience, who identified themselves as Dutch Neo-Calvinists, that Kuyper called the Trek of the Dutch Reformers "a power evoked by God that will *(would)* dominate the total future of Africa and partly even the history of the world."[5]

While the Dutch Reformers dominated the nation-building program of the 1940s, Mandela's nation building is the responsibility of both black and Dutch Reformers. To continue my metaphorical use of the notions "black" and "white," allow me to repeat myself. President Mandela, and through him the whole country,

5. J. D. Du Toit, "De Geschiedenis Der Hollandse Kerken in Zuid-Africa," in T. Hamersam, ed., *De Geschiedenis Van De Christelike Kerk* (Potchefstroom: Het Western Drukkerij, 1911), pp. 267-375.

expects the delivery of the new society also from "Dutch" Reformers and "black" Reformers, however divided they now may be.

The vital question is whether Reformed faith, and these two divided Reformed communities, will play their rightful transformative role in the project of nation building. Another vital question is how these communities will be able to participate in nation building. Christian higher education will be challenged to come to terms with this new moment of truth for Reformed people in South Africa. This must be possible if we are prepared not only to keep the Reformed faith but to seek the new calling of Calvinism in our context. Meeting this presidential challenge indeed requires a journey, a move. I would like to refer to three great moves that both Dutch Reformers and black Reformers are required to make in the interest of nation building. Thereafter, I would like to draw your attention to a number of additional national challenges these divided Reformed communities will have to face in the pursuit of nation building. I hope that you will understand my use of "Dutch" and Reformed over against "black" and Reformed as mere metaphors describing the total South African reality. My story is also the tale of two traditions and two churches.

Moving from Babelism to Ubuntufication

Let us talk about the first move that "whites" and "blacks" are required to make. The most poignant difference between the international debate on community as a metaphor for nation building and the South African quest is that the former represents a move away from individualism while the latter constitutes a move away from Babelism. The Old Testament story of the building of the Tower of Babel features prominently among the classical texts of the theology of apartheid. This Genesis 11 story was interpreted as the divine sanction for human division along racial, language, and cultural lines. Babel became the operating metaphor and the organizing principle for apartheid. The story of Babel gave rise to an ideology that I denote as Babelism. Our task is to find our way from Babelism to ubuntufication. *Ubuntu* is an African word meaning "moral community." Its point of departure is that a person is a person only because of and among other persons.

In accordance with this ideal, Archbishop Desmond Tutu aptly suggested "that the West might consider a small gift we in Africa just could offer. It is the gift of *ubuntu* — a term difficult to translate into occidental languages. But it is the essence of being human, it declares that my humanity is caught up and inextricably bound up in yours. . . . I am because I belong."[6]

This move from Babel to ubuntu obviously brings its own diversity of perspectives: the perspective from above (high anthropology) and the perspective from below (low anthropology). According to the view from below it forms a move from "non personhood" to "being in community." In the perspective from above it constitutes a reduction in the standards of being, including everything that defined "white personhood." Dutch Reformers and black Reformers are challenged to develop a just and humane theological anthropology that can subvert the reality of racial "high" and "low" anthropologies that resulted from Babelism.

Moving from Kuyper to Belhar

The second move with which Dutch Reformers and black Reformers will have to contend is the move from Kuyper to Belhar. John de Gruchy defines Dutch Reformers as "the product of an uneasy amalgam of nineteenth-century evangelical piety and an adapted Kuyperian neo-Calvinism forged on the fires of the Afrikaner struggle for cultural identity and political and economic power." He therefore sees Afrikaner Calvinism as "an aberration of Calvinism."[7]

While past disagreements between the Dutch Reformers and the black Reformers centered on the theology of Abraham Kuyper, the more recent struggles are focusing on the Confession of Belhar. The first phase of the struggle was eloquently represented by church leaders such as Johan Heyns, the late Dutch Reformed

---

6. T. F. Best and G. Gassman, eds., *On the Way to a Fuller Koinonia: Official Report of the Fifth World Council on Faith and Order* (Geneva: World Council of Churches, 1993), pp. 93-102.

7. Smit, "Reformed Theology," pp. xvi, 29.

leader, and Allan Boesak, the erstwhile black Reformed leader. While the Dutch Reformers called on Abraham Kuyper to justify apartheid, the black Reformers accused them of "abusing" Kuyper's theology.[8]

The Confession of Belhar was adopted by the Dutch Reformed Mission Church as the result of the declaration of some *status confessionis* with regard to the theological justification of apartheid by the Dutch Reformed Church. It was recently reenacted as the fourth Confession of the Uniting Reformed Church in Southern Africa. Its true significance stems from the fact that it made the ethical commitment to justice central to faith, confession, and the unity of the church. The Confession of Belhar is a witness to the fact that this church understood its political and ecclesiastical task as a matter of faithfulness in following Jesus of Nazareth.

Chris Loff is of the opinion that the only difference between the Belgic Confession and the Heidelberg Catechism (HK) on the one hand and the Confession of Belhar on the other is that the latter deals with only one confessional issue, namely, the way the Dutch Reformed Mission Church understands the concept of church (ecclesiology).[9] I differ with Loff because to my mind it is theology (the contextual question of God) as it relates to Christology (the contextual question of Jesus Christ) that forms the central matter of the Confession of Belhar. Indeed, this christological focus is related to the issue of church unity, but the latter does not form the center. The actual dynamic of the Confession of Belhar is the establishment of a direct connection between the reconciling, uniting, and liberating acts of God and the praxeology of the believers. Durand argues for the confession in the midst of the ecumenical

8. There is an ongoing debate on the status of Kuyperian theology in South Africa. Largely a debate among white thinkers, it does not have much impact on the theme of this paper, which seeks the connection between "Dutch" and "black" Reformed discourses. See P. J. Strauss, "Abraham Kuyper, Apartheid and Reformed Churches in South Africa in Their Support of Apartheid," *REC Theological Forum* 23 (March 1995): 1-11; John de Gruchy, *Liberating Reformed Theology* (Grand Rapids: Eerdmans, 1991); W. A. de Klerk, *The Puritans in Africa* (London: Rex, 1984); A. J. Botha, *Die Evolusie Van 'N Volksteologie* (Bellville, South Africa: University of the Western Cape Press, 1984).

9. "Die N G Sendingkerk en Kerkeenheid," *Apologia* 2 (August 1990): 2-9.

debate that calls for the subjugation of the word-confession to the confessional deed. He believed that the heretical nature of the context of South Africa at the time required a confessional word that could result in deeds.[10] De Gruchy, who regarded the Confession of Belhar as the result of black theology, goes further by stating that its significance stems from the fact that ethical commitment becomes the center of faith and confession.[11]

It is my understanding that Belhar must be heard as a herald of the deed (praxis) and not as affirmation of an orthodoxy. The final word of the confession is not about "the right belief." The ultimate language of Belhar is the language of obedience and the following of Jesus of Nazareth (discipleship): "We believe that, in obedience to Jesus Christ, its only Head, the Church is called to confess and to do all these things, even though the authorities and human laws might forbid them and punishment and suffering be the consequence." The call to discipleship is praxeological in intent and content. The conflict is wrongly regarded as the struggle between orthodoxy and orthopraxis. The direct biblical relationship between faith and praxis subverts such juxtapositioning. However, from this interrelatedness of faith and praxis emerge the doxological needs to put it in words. Smit clarifies this point sufficiently when he argues in favor of the idea that the Confession of Belhar is a doxological way of glorifying the acts of God in the face of the argument of Sauter.[12] Sauter believed that such a direct connection between theology and ethics would lead to an unacceptable short-circuiting of knowledge and of argumentation.

The Confession of Belhar has become the new area of theological conflict and concern on the way to church unity. The Dutch Reformers find it impossible to accept the Confession of Belhar. Decisions of the Western Cape Synod of the Dutch Reformed Church in South Africa on Saturday, 21 October 1995, again confirmed this. The synod decided to conclude with a mere "we identify

---

10. "'n Belydenis — Was Dit Regtig Nodig," in D. J. Smit and G. D. Cloete, eds., *Moment of Truth* (Grand Rapids: Eerdmans, 1984), p. 39.
11. G. Loots, ed., *Listening to South African Voices: Critical Reflection on Contemporary Theological Documents* (Cape Town: Woordkor, 1990), pp. 13-14.
12. Smit and Cloete, *Moment of Truth*, pp. 141-43.

(vereenselwig) with the Confession of Belhar." This is the furthest that the white Dutch Reformed ethos is prepared to go. But this is not enough: To identify with is profoundly different from being identified by. Why do we have this deadlock? At issue is the belief in God as "the God of justice" who sides with the poor and the oppressed. Although Nick Wolterstorff argued convincingly that the embrace of justice and peace is by nature the concern of Reformed theology, this remains a controversial matter for Reformed Christians in South Africa. While the Dutch Reformers speak only about a God of compassion who deals justly, black Reformers identify God as the God of justice.

We have expressed our deepest faith convictions in the following word of the Belhar Confession:

> We believe that God has revealed himself as the One who wishes to bring about justice and true peace among people; that in a world full of injustice and enmity He is in a special way the God of the destitute, the poor and the wronged and that He calls his Church to follow Him in this; that He brings justice to the oppressed and gives bread to the hungry; that He frees the prisoner and restores sight to the blind; that He supports the downtrodden, protects the stranger, helps orphans and widows and blocks the path of the ungodly; that for Him pure and undefiled religion is to visit the orphans and the widows in their suffering; that He wishes to teach His people to do what is good and to seek the right;
>
> that the Church must therefore stand by people in any form of suffering and need, which implies, among other things, that the Church must witness against and strive against any form of injustice, so that justice may roll down like waters, and righteousness like an ever-flowing stream;
>
> that the Church as the possession of God must stand where He stands, namely against injustice and with the wronged; that in following Christ the Church must witness against all the powerful and privileged who selfishly seek their own interests and thus control and harm others.

Therefore we reject any ideology which would legitimate forms of injustice and any doctrine which is unwilling to resist such an ideology in the name of the gospel. (Belhar Confession 1986; for the text, see Cloete and Smit 1984)

Discourse in South African Calvinism will be moving from Kuyper to Belhar in the interest of the nation-building project. But this is not the only journey we are required to make. We are also called to move from *doing* theology to *being theological*.

Moving from Doing Theology to Story Telling

Robert Schreiter quickly found that the political violence of apartheid was an attempt "to destroy the narratives that sustain people's identities and substitute narratives of its own." He calls the latter "narratives of the lie," narratives of negation. The negation was not only meant to destroy the narrative of the victim, but to pave the way for the oppressor's narrative. However, human beings cannot survive without narratives. In fact, they survive through their memories wrapped up in stories. Their healing comes from narratives. Schreiter correctly concludes by saying, "To trivialize and ignore memory is to trivialize and ignore human identity, and to trivialize and ignore human identity is to trivialize and ignore human dignity."[13]

Therefore, the ethics of being — or what Stanley Hauerwas calls the ethics of character — is gaining dominance in South African theological circles. The central question is not "What or how are we called to be?" but "Who are we called to be?" in the new South Africa. This is a very important shift that is taking place. It requires us to face up to our memories, the narrative structure of what we call "Dutch" and Reformed as well as the narratives of what we call "black" and Reformed.

Schreiter warns us that

13. R. J. Schreiter, *Reconciliation: Mission and Ministry in a Changing Social Order* (New York: Orbis, 1992), p. 34.

The reconstruction of memory, however, is not simply a retrieval of memory. That old memory becomes so associated with violence that it becomes too painful to evoke. What must be done to overcome this suffering is to disengage the older memory from those acts of violence. That is done by repeating the narrative of the violence over and over again to ease the burden of trauma that it carries. Such an activity begins to put a boundary around the violence, as it was, to separate it from the memory. For that reason memory must be reconstructed. It will never be the same again; it will bear the scars of its history.[14]

Having looked at the main journeys we will have to make in the interest of justice and the Reformed integrity, I now would like to highlight three obstacles to overcome on the way to each other, namely, language, irreconcilability, and massive poverty. These obstacles have become part of a national strategy to overcome the legacy of apartheid. I will therefore refer to the proposed instruments of change in talking about the obstacles.

The Problem of Moral Language

If storytelling is the way toward nation building, we will undoubtedly be confronted with the problem of moral language. Babelism is a metaphor that implies "confusion of speech" or simply a problem of language. South Africans have been talking to each other over the many decades of apartheid. We have discovered that we are actually speaking past each other, that we do not understand each other. We hear people speaking to each other with conflicting assumptions, opposing worldviews, and contesting emotions. During the negotiation process the politicians used more time on "talks about talks" before they could finally negotiate a settlement. Much of the violence of our country has to do with the problem of moral language. Violence is a distorted form of language. It is the clearest sign that we do not yet have a common moral language. Theologians from the erstwhile apartheid divide are now charged

14. Ibid., p. 12.

with the responsibility to give theological leadership in the time between the times. This is the most awesome responsibility that one could imagine.

Habermas once described the greatest "pathology of modernity" as a double alienation. First there is the alienation of subject specialists from one another, and then there is the alienation of specialists from the everyday lives of people. Theologians do not understand each other, and the ordinary citizens experience them as not speaking the language of the person on the street.[15] How will it be possible for theologians to contribute to nation building if this is the case? The situation is considerably worsened by Wesley Kort's conclusion that Christians are bound to differ. He found that the positions, traditions, and theologies of Christians are formed by their differences. Kort argued that oppositional relationships are necessary vehicles of ecclesial forms. In fact, he argued that Christians are "bound to differ" — in his book with the same title. He then went on to say that Christian churches "establish their identities, their power and meaning, by means of differences from and opposition to other churches."[16] This holds true for the South African situation as well. Dutch Reformers and black Reformers experience themselves as in oppositional relationships. Together, they suffer from the double alienation. We have to overcome this. We have to grow into a covenantal relationship.

Theologians have serious disabilities to overcome if theology is to be of any real meaning in the South African context. The demythologizing of theology is urgently needed. The leveling of the playing field to empower the prophecy and the priesthood of believers is a real challenge. The theological search for an African ecclesiology for the public church is beginning to take shape. It is yet too early to know where we are heading. But we are in the Kuhnian paradigm switch. We have only just entered the pre-

15. D. J. Smit, *Etiek na Babel?* Unpublished paper in possession of the author.

16. Wesley Kort, *Bound to Differ: The Dynamic of Theological Discourse* (University Park: Pennsylvania State University Press, 1992), p. 26. See also D. J. Smit, "The Symbol of Reconciliation in an Ideological Conflict," in W. S. Vorster, ed., *Reconciliation and Construction* (Pretoria, South Africa: UNISA, 1986), pp. 2-14.

paradigmatic phase and many different and at times conflicting proposals are being investigated. The formation of a new conscious-ness of belonging is at the heart of this search. The quest is for local faith communities to become public spaces where people who once were enemies could meet, a space for listening and for sharing stories. Dr. Kistner, the well-known ecumenical theologian who works with Beyers Naudé, said in this regard that

> Churches should devote great care towards facilitating opportuni-ties for encounter and fellowship between the perpetrators and the victims of oppression during the apartheid regime and assist them to exchange their stories and experiences and fears with the view to a process of mutual acceptance and forgiveness. The society and the religious or an ideological community or cultural group which has contributed towards shaping the mind of the offender shares in the responsibility of the offence and is in need of repentance on its part and forgiveness on the part of God and the victims with the view to facilitating a process of healing and taking precautions against a repetition of the offence.[17]

This means that the Dutch Reformers and the black Reformers will have the most awesome task of talking to each other as per-petrators and victims of apartheid in the interest of truth and reconciliation. Structural unity is necessary for the creation of space for narratives.

This brings us to one of the most important instruments in coming to terms with our past identity in forging the way for a new South African identity: The Truth and Reconciliation Commission.

The Problem of Truth and Reconciliation

At present all the roads of new beginnings in South Africa seem to lead through the very controversial Truth and Reconciliation Com-mission. The growing consensus of some of the South African Chris-

17. W. Kistner, *The Legacy of the Past in South Africa* (Pretoria, South Africa: South African Council of Churches, 1994).

tian groups is that such a commission will be a crucial national symbol. It will be the place where a new moral judgment on apartheid is established and a new moral commitment to the future is forged. The central hope of people is that the Truth and Reconciliation Commission will bring forth a shared reading of the past, a common language about the past, communal heroes, and rituals of reconciliation.

The responses of Christians to the idea of the Truth and Reconciliation Commission can be divided into five groups. The first group are those who are fundamentally opposed to the idea. For them the most important thing to do is to forget about apartheid so that they can get on with their lives. However, we know that victims have a long memory and they continue to carry the unforgettable scars of their suffering. On the other hand, those who caused that suffering have short memories. They seemingly do not know the extent of what they have done and they also do not want to know. There is only one real memory left and that is the memory of the wounded. Therefore, I want to share with you in more detail the four other responses. These responses represent the Research Institute on Christianity at the University of Cape Town, the position of the faculty of Religion and Theology at the University of the Western Cape, the church leaders under the flag of the South African Council of Churches, and an uncoordinated group of critical theologians.

The response from the University of Cape Town describes the Truth and Reconciliation Commission as a national care process. "It will show that the nation cares."[18] Its point of departure is that all the people of South Africa have suffered irreparably from the history of this country. As such the Truth and Reconciliation Commission has a pastoral function with regard to the victims as well as the perpetrators. The grand motive for this pastoral process is the restoration of the people's humanity.

For this purpose the task of the commission is described as

> establishing and making known the fate or whereabouts of the
> victims of gross violations of human rights and by restoring the

18. *Memorandum of the Research Institute on Christianity in South Africa,* 1994, pp. 1-2.

human and civil dignity of such victims by granting them an opportunity to relate their own accounts of the violations of which they are the victims, by recommending reparation measures in respect of them (cf. the Green paper of Parliament on the Truth and Reconciliation Commission).[19]

The Church Leaders Consultation of the SACC agrees that the Truth and Reconciliation Commission is a national symbol. They differ from the UCT viewpoint in that they do not see the commission as a symbol of care. They perceive it to be a legal symbol. The commission represents a symbol on which pastoral action can, nevertheless, capitalize. The central pastoral aim is described as "making our memories redemptive": "We as the religious community take a separate but parallel responsibility to the commission . . . before, during and after this process."[20] They then declare that the pastoral function belongs by nature to the church. Consequently they identify five stages of pastoral action proper in which the religious community should be involved:

1. Helping the nation to come to terms with the past as well as to move from the old to the new;
2. Providing for counseling and confession, or pre-disclosure guidance or counseling;
3. Offering a ministry of accompaniment of the confessant to the room of confession, in this case the Truth Commission;
4. Affecting the priestly liturgical function of atonement to help the nation to accept the reality of the past and develop corrective measures to ensure that those experiences are never repeated;
5. Accompanying the nation into a new life, a new experience, a new culture, and a new morality.

The response of a number of theologians at the University of the Western Cape supports the position of the church leaders on the

19. Ibid.
20. *Recommendations from the Church Leaders Consultation,* 12 August 1994, pp. 1-4.

proper and separate responsibility of pastoral care. Yes, the Truth and Reconciliation Commission is a national legal symbol. They go even further to identify a narrow legal focus, namely, the contravention of human rights. These theologians of the University of the Western Cape acknowledge the ligitimacy of such an approach. However, the church's responsibility, they maintain, goes beyond the concern for the contravention of human rights by individuals. The church is pastorally concerned about truth and reconciliation. As such, they say, the church would understand that the government has to close the human rights book on the past. But the pastoral care book cannot be closed.

There is indeed a fourth group of theologians who argue, from a more critical basis, that the process should be "about the truth and nothing but the truth," that is, the *truth* and not reconciliation should be the primary concern of the process. Their point of departure is that the commission is a legal and political instrument. It will investigate a crime against humanity. The point of departure for the investigation must be the biblical preferential option for the victims of apartheid and colonialism. This calls for a moral and legal separation of those who suffered under apartheid and colonialism and those who supported it. A legal equilateral treatment of opposing forces and supporters of apartheid will lead to a distortion of historical facts.

Although it is important to give the latter viewpoint its due regard, the legal and political reality already dictates a reconciliatory truth-seeking process. This may be the price we have to pay for the kind of transition we had to negotiate. Charles Villa-Vicencio correctly stated that

> Perhaps the most important contribution that religion can realistically make as the country struggles to find new direction, is the promotion of a sense of national catharsis. It is to assist the nation to "put the lights on" and to admit the extent to which it has violated the humanity of its people. It is to enable the nation to turn away from the past to a fundamentally different kind of future.[21]

21. Charles M. Villa-Vicencio, "Keeping the Revolution Human: Religion and Reconstruction," *Journal for the Study of Religion* 6 (1993): 49-68.

Truth and Reconciliation Alone Are Not Enough

The risk of falling into the trap of false reconciliation is also at stake, as Robert Schreiter warns. Schreiter identifies three types of false reconciliation: (a) reconciliation as a hasty peace; (b) reconciliation that does not lead to liberation; (c) reconciliation as a managed process. To avoid the first pitfall we need the Truth Commission. To steer away from a false reconciliation that does not lead to liberation and becomes simply a matter of conflict management we need the Reconstruction and Development Programme.

On the basis of this vision the black Reformers and sectors of the Dutch Reformers are now affirming and supporting, with so many other South Africans, the Reconstruction and Development Programme (RDP) of the South African government. The Government's White Paper on "Reconstruction and Development" (15 November 1994) provides impetus for the RDP, as the following quotations indicate:

> Our history has been a bitter one dominated by colonialism, racism, apartheid, sexism and repressive labour practices. The result is that poverty and degradation exist side by side with modern cities and developed mining, industrial and commercial infrastructure. Our income distribution is racially distorted and ranks as one of the most unequal in the world. Women are still subject to innumerable forms of discrimination and bias. Rural people and youth are marginalised. A combination of lavish wealth and abject poverty characterises our society.

> The economy was built on systematically enforced racial division in every sphere. Rural areas were divided into underdeveloped Bantustans and well-developed, white-owned commercial farming areas; towns and cities were divided into townships without basic infrastructure for blacks and well-resourced suburbs for whites. Segregation in education, health, welfare, transport and employment left deep scars of inequality and economic inefficiency. Violence has had a devastating effect on our society and the need to restore peace and a sense of community security, is paramount.

In commerce and industry, very large conglomerates dominated by whites control large parts of the economy. Cheap labour policies and employment segregation have concentrated skills in white hands. Workers are poorly equipped for the rapid changes taking place in the world economy. Small and medium-sized enterprises are underdeveloped, while highly protected industries lower investment in research, development and training. The informal sector and "survival sector" include many of South Africa's women workers, who are underpaid and exploited.

The result is that in every sphere of our society — economic, social, legal, political, moral, cultural, environmental — South Africans are confronted by serious problems. . . .

At the same time, the challenges facing South Africa are enormous. Only a comprehensive approach to harnessing the resources of our country can reverse the crisis created by apartheid.

No political democracy can survive and flourish if the majority of its people remains in poverty, without land, without their basic needs being met and without tangible prospects for a better life. Attacking poverty and deprivation is the first priority of the democratic Government.

How can we do this successfully? A programme is required that is achievable, sustainable and meets the objectives of freedom, and an improved standard of living and quality of life for all South Africans within a peaceful and stable society characterised by equitable economic growth.

It is clear that the RDP is a collective attempt to meet the basic needs of poor people, to abolish discrimination on grounds of race, class, and gender, to redress the past policies of exploitation and repression, and to reverse the distortions in the economy that adversely affect the poor. The emphasis is on growth and on progress. It is not a welfare program, but a program of empowerment: It is "a vision for the fundamental transformation of our society." The most difficult obstacle for the church to overcome in supporting the vision of the Reconstruction and Development Programme is to join forces in the RDP forums, to fulfill its calling in partnership with nongovernmental organizations, local communities, and local government.

A Partnership

Neither the Dutch Reformers nor the black Reformers can boast the final word on the formation of society. They will have to join society in a healing cycle of transformation. No clear lines are to be drawn between societal metaphors and ecclesial metaphors. A new language, understood by those in the church as well as by those outside, will have to evolve. I hope that the day that Dietrich Bonhoeffer dreamed of (cf. his thoughts about the baptism of Dietrich Bethge, May 1944) will soon dawn: the day when the people of South Africa will once again be called to speak the Word of God in such a way that the world is changed by it. We yearn for the dawn of a new language, perhaps, as Dietrich Bonhoeffer suggested, totally areligious but indeed liberating and redeeming as the language of Jesus Christ, by Almighty God and through the Holy Spirit. Indeed, it will disturb the people, but they will eventually surrender to the self-validity enshrined in its message and actions. This is the kind of Kairos that gives birth to what Wolterstorff calls world-formative Christianity.[22]

We are, however, at times tempted to indulge in the luxury of otherworldly theologies. We sometimes want to say "No!" to the calling of nation building. We do have a choice to go into the desert of withdrawal from the real issues of the social world. It may even be easier for both Dutch Reformers and black Reformers to remain in their various homelands. But we cannot escape our theological responsibility to "those to whom the future belongs" in obedience to God. The very existence of the generation of the future constitutes an "ethos of responsibility" defined in terms of the future. The theolog-

22. Nicholas Wolterstorff, *Until Justice and Peace Embrace* (Grand Rapids: Eerdmans, 1983).

ical quest of any generation must never forget the generation to whom the future belongs. Bonhoeffer aptly reminded us that

> The ultimate question for a responsible man to ask is not how he is to extricate himself heroically from the affair, but how the coming generation is to live. It is only from this question, with its responsibility towards (coming) history, that fruitful solutions can come, even if for the time being they are very humiliating. Indeed, it is much easier to see a thing through from the point of view of abstract principle than from that of concrete responsibility. The rising generation will always instinctively discern which of these we make the basis of our actions, for it is their own future that is at stake.[23]

Dutch Reformers and black Reformers will have to come to terms with their Reformed commitment to participate in the transformation of the new society. Given the history of apartheid, we, collectively, are morally obligated to assist in the birth of a nation, a nation coming from the experience of an extraordinary human disaster that lasted far too long.

I want to conclude with the last words in Bonhoeffer's sermon on "Thy Kingdom Come." He reminds people in situations of transformation and reorientation about a strange story from the Old Testament. This story has all the markings of the theological quest of the Dutch Reformers and the black Reformers in South Africa. Jacob, says Bonhoeffer, fled from his home and lived for many years in a foreign country in a state of enmity with his brother. Then the urge to return home and to his brother became insistent. He discovered later that it was only a small river that separated him from his brother. As he prepared to cross the river, he was stopped. A stranger wrestled with him. From this struggle a blessing was born: the sunrise!

> Then the sun rises on Jacob, and he proceeds into the promised land, limping because his thigh has been put out of joint. The

23. Dietrich Bonhoeffer, *Letters and Papers from Prison* (New York: Macmillan, 1972), p. 7.

way is clear; the dark door to the land of promise has been broken open. The blessing has come from out of the curse, and now the sun shines upon him. That the way of all of us into the land of promise leads through the night; that we also enter it as those who are perhaps curiously scarred from the struggle with God, the struggle for his kingdom and his grace; and that we enter the land of God and of our brother [and sister] as limping warriors — all these things we Christians have in common with Jacob. And we know that the sun is destined also for us, and this knowledge allows us to bear with patience the time of wandering and waiting and believing that is imposed upon us. But beyond Jacob, we know something else. We know it is not we who must go; we know that He comes to us. . . . That is why we pray, "Thy kingdom come to us."[24]

24. Ibid.

"You Talkin' to Me?":
The Christian Liberal Arts Tradition
and the Challenge of Popular Culture

William D. Romanowski

O n one of my first visits to Calvin College, I joined several professors for lunch in the Faculty/Staff Dining Room. During introductions, I related my interest in popular culture studies, which was greeted with some snickering, and a joke about students flocking to such courses. But as conversations go, one comment led to another, and suddenly we were talking about the television series *Hill Street Blues,* which was at its peak of popularity then. It became immediately obvious to me that this program was part of their weekly ritual; they were very informed about even small details. Here were these "scholars" conversing (and at points even arguing) about characters and episodes they liked or disliked, changes they noted in the handling of themes over several seasons, the gritty texture of the series, the quality of acting and writing. Then all at

I have explored these issues in greater detail and depth in two publications in press: *Pop Culture Wars: Religion and the Role of Entertainment in American Life* (Downers Grove: InterVarsity Press, 1996); and "John Calvin Meets the Creature from the Black Lagoon: The Christian Reformed Church and the Movies 1928-1966," *Christian Scholar's Review* 25 (September 1995): 47-62. I am grateful to the two publishers for their permission to place my ideas in this context. — W.D.R.

once the conversation stopped, as if they had forgotten and suddenly remembered my presence. One professor said, "Of course, I always read a book while I'm watching it."

Popular culture may be "the ultimate instance of American mixed feelings," as a writer in *Time* magazine put it.[1] On the one hand, popular culture, and entertainment in particular, has been criticized as trivial, mindless, and escapist amusement. On other occasions (and we are in the midst of one now), attacks on popular culture range from charges of debasement of taste to the destruction of values, with critics charging that popular culture wields an influence that could potentially overwhelm the combined efforts of family, church, and school to shape our society. But something cannot be trivial and dangerous at the same time; it is either one or the other. Capable of enthralling audiences around the world, setting fashions, selling products, and communicating ideas, the entertainment media and popular culture industries are today recognized as being among our most active and vital cultural processes.

College students, and those at Calvin are no exception, live and learn in a social, cultural, and material environment that is highly influenced by the popular culture industries. Radios, televisions, and VCRs are standard features of dormitory rooms. Movies shown on campus regularly attract hundreds of students. The gym is always packed on Homecoming weekend for the annual ritual celebration of student life at Calvin — Airband. The Bruce Cockburn concert was a sellout; students camped out overnight in midwinter to be first in line for tickets to a Hootie and the Blowfish concert. Members of the Grand Rapids community, and especially our African-American neighbors, joined Calvin faculty, staff, and alumni at the recent Buckshot LeFonque (featuring Branford Marsalis) concert

---

1. Jay Cocks, "Pop Goes the Culture," *Time,* 16 June 1986, p. 68. Popular culture and entertainment lack precise definition. I am using "popular" broadly, referring to the products of work and thought, mass-produced or disseminated by the mass media, that are characteristic of a large population or group. For the purposes of this essay my illustrations are drawn specifically from entertainment. For a fuller discussion see "What Is the History of Popular Culture," *History Today* 3 (December 1985): 39-45; Richard Maltby, ed., *Passing Parade: A History of Popular Culture in the Twentieth Century* (New York: Oxford University Press, 1989); Richard Dyer, *Only Entertainment* (New York: Routledge, 1992).

in the Fine Arts Auditorium; Calvin students danced on the floor where synod delegates meet annually. Not surprisingly, a recent report from the provost's office listed popular culture among the forces shaping higher education today, while also noting that "Education is lagging behind in the redesign of American institutions."[2] But how is it that although popular culture is perceived as a powerful force in our world, it has until recently been excluded from serious treatment by educational institutions?

American popular culture is as old as the colonies, but the appearance of high and popular culture as distinctive categories in American life occurred around the turn of this century, just as the movies, the phonograph, and, later, the radio were born. The means of communication and cultural transmission in the new mass society became critical arenas in the cultural conflict at the beginning of this century, just as they are in our contemporary culture wars.

Long before the high and low disjunction in American life, however, the church condemned spectacle entertainment as such, establishing a path the Christian Reformed Church (CRC) followed in its response to "worldly amusements." The high and low bifurcation continues to affect the cultural dialogue, and it is worthwhile examining its influence in the Reformed tradition. Wrestling with this burden out of our past can lead to a distinctive Reformed contribution to the contemporary discussion about popular culture. Treatment of popular culture today is not just some multicultural faddishness, but reveals a historic passion in the church that dates back to its beginnings, as well as to the confluence of religious, cultural, and social forces in American life.

*   *   *

The turn of this century was marked by a profound transformation in American society. Americans were aware that they were living in a new age that was being created by the combined forces of modernism — rapid industrialism and urbanization, the rise of individu-

---

2. "Reformed Christian Higher Education for a Changing World: A Strategic Plan for Calvin College, 1995-2000," January 1995.

alism, and the advent of a mass society. Fueled by the huge influx of non–English-speaking immigrants from Europe and Asia and African-Americans migrating from the South, the northern industrial cities were rapidly becoming multiethnic, multicultural, and multilingual centers of work and amusement.[3] Immigrants were expected to pass through an assimilationist "melting pot," leaving their language, ethnic, and cultural traditions behind in order to embrace the ways of their adoptive country. But at least one college president wondered if the new immigrants would "become a part of the body politic, and firm supporters of liberal institutions, or will they prove to our republic what the Goths and Huns were to the Roman Empire?"[4]

The realities of the urban-industrial society undermined the dominant Victorian culture of the prosperous Anglo-American Protestant groups who saw the new consumer-oriented values as fundamentally and socially destructive. Rapid social transformation created a conflict that cultural historian Warren Susman described as a struggle between the older "producer-capitalist culture, and a newly emerging culture of abundance. . . . The battle was between

3. Urban areas increased from 28 to 52 percent of the population between the Civil War and 1920. Lary May, *Screening Out the Past: The Birth of Mass Culture and the Motion Picture Industry* (Chicago: University of Chicago Press, 1989), p. 29.

4. The president of Middlebury College, quoted in *Education in the United States: A Documentary History*, vol. 2, ed. Sol Cohen (New York: Random House, n.d.), p. 995. Restrictions in the early 1920s reduced the flow of immigration to a trickle as a way of protecting capitalism and democracy from foreign ideologies, and "keeping pure the blood of America," as one House representative put it. Quoted in Ted Howard and Jeremy Rifkin, *Who Should Play God?* (New York: Dell, 1977), p. 69. There were other related problems for Anglo-Americans after the Civil War, when conquest of the frontier was renewed. By 1890, however, the Indian population had been reduced from an estimated original 1.5 million to under 250,000, and the Indian nations were colonized on restricted reservations. The Compromise of 1877 reasserted the political hegemony of southern Whites; the 1896 Supreme Court decision *Plessy v. Ferguson* established the doctrine of "equal but separate" facilities for African-Americans. Arrell Morgan Gibson, *The American Indian: Prehistory to the Present* (Lexington: D. C. Heath and Company, 1980), p. 443; C. Vann Woodward, *Reunion and Reaction: The Compromise of 1877 and the End of Reconstruction* (Boston: Little, Brown and Company, 1951).

rival perceptions of the world, different visions of life."[5] From a wide range of perspectives there was a shared sense that American civilization was in a crisis.

In their quest to maintain control over institutional life and the national culture, the American Victorians were influenced by European intellectual trends, including Darwin's evolutionary theory and ideas about culture that came from the literary Romantic tradition of Coleridge, Carlyle, and especially Matthew Arnold.[6] When Arnold arrived in the United States for a lecture tour in 1883, he was greeted by Andrew Carnegie, one of the nation's leading industrialists, and hosted by the most prominent and wealthy citizens on the eastern seaboard. Arnold's ideas about culture suited the Victorians, justifying the fragmentation of American life already taking place, and the separation of the wealthy and educated elite from the industrial masses.

Arnold defined *Culture* as the "pursuit of our total perfection by means of getting to know, on all the matters which most concern us, the best which has been thought and said in the world."[7] Culture was a goal, an ideal, an "internal condition" of the mind characterized by an individual process of intellectual, aesthetic, and spiritual refinement. Culture not only distinguished humans from their "animality," but those who pursued Culture reached a higher level of humanity than the "raw and uncultivated" masses. The term, as he used it, referred specifically to human perfection and the highest human achievements, which for Arnold and his followers culminated in the historically developed refinement of British and European high culture. It was as though cultural development was finished, however, rather than an ongoing, dynamic process. Culture, then, was to be distinguished from the human thought and

5. Warren I. Susman, *Culture as History: The Transformation of American Society in the Twentieth Century* (New York: Pantheon Books, 1984), p. xx.

6. See Raymond Williams, "Culture," in *Keywords: A Vocabulary of Culture and Society* (New York: Oxford University Press, 1976), pp. 76-82; Chris Jenks, *Culture* (New York: Routledge, 1993).

7. Matthew Arnold, *Culture and Anarchy*, ed. J. Dover Wilson (Cambridge, England: Cambridge University Press, 1932; reprint 1988). The quoted material is taken from pp. 6, 47, 76, 95, 204. *Culture and Anarchy* was first published in 1869, with revised editions appearing in 1875 and 1882.

products of "civilization," or what Arnold perceived as the corrosive effects of industrialization and mass society.

Arnold's concept of culture was thoroughly humanistic. The pursuit of Culture deified reason and subsumed religion, replacing the Holy-Spirited process of sanctification.[8] Culture became an evolutionary scheme, a "faith in the progress of humanity towards perfection," intended to maintain a privileged class of "best selves" among the educated minority who would be the supreme arbiters of Culture.

The Victorians already thought of themselves as the most advanced in the evolutionary scheme and leaders in the progress of civilization. Arnoldian Culture became the basis for a cultural hegemony as a bulwark against societal anarchy; Anglo-American high culture was to be preserved, protected, and aspired toward by all. As Lawrence Levine pointed out, however, this "led the arbiters of culture on the one hand to insulate themselves from the masses in order to promote and preserve pure culture, and on the other to reach out to the masses and sow the seeds of culture among them in order to ensure civilized order."[9] As Levine and others have shown, a "cultural hierarchy" emerged; American culture was divided into high and low, or elite and popular culture as a primary means of social, intellectual, and aesthetic separation.[10]

8. Neo-Calvinist scholar Henry R. Van Til called Arnold's faith in Hellenistic culture "pathetic," and criticized his idea of culture as "thoroughly humanistic, man-centered." The principial flaw in Arnold's work was that he attributed to the intellect and reason that which belonged to the more fundamental religious impulse of humans. Arnold "failed to accept the biblical doctrine that the issues of life are out of the heart. . . . He is accordingly basically sub-Christian in his thinking," Van Til wrote. Henry R. Van Til, *The Calvinistic Concept of Culture* (Grand Rapids: Baker Book House, 1959), pp. 26-27.

9. Lawrence Levine, *Highbrow/Lowbrow: The Emergence of Cultural Hierarchy in America* (Cambridge: Harvard University Press, 1988), p. 206. Daniel Walker Howe thought that the reification of high and low culture was actually a "symptom of the disintegration of Victorian culture," diminishing the influence of the Victorians over the public opinion of the masses and creating an animosity between the classes. Daniel Walker Howe, "Victorian Culture in America," in *Victorian America,* ed. Daniel Walker Howe (Philadelphia: University of Pennsylvania Press, 1976), p. 14.

10. See Levine, *Highbrow/Lowbrow;* David Grimsted, *Melodrama Unveiled: American Theater and Culture 1800-1850* (Chicago: University of Chicago Press, 1968); Paul DiMaggio, "Cultural Entrepreneurship in Nineteeth-Century Bos-

For our purposes here, there are two important consequences of the reification of high and low culture as it delineated the traditional high arts from contemporary popular art forms with different institutions and standards. First, the traditional high arts were divorced from any meaningful purpose in the everyday lives of most people. As Nicholas Wolterstorff observed, this "is characteristic neither of institutions of art in other societies nor of our own society's total institution of art."[11] Historically, the arts have served multiple purposes, and achieve their status by the way they function and are used, and the social institutions within which works are produced, distributed and consumed. The high arts, however, existed now only for aesthetic "disinterested" contemplation.[12] As a result, "legitimate" theater, opera, symphony, and museums struggled to survive financially and were funded by a patronage system (and later public funding through government agencies) that further distanced these forms from the general audience, while also restricting the role of social institutions in the emerging popular culture industries.

Second, and conversely, with the emergence of twentieth-century mass culture, popular art forms increasingly served roles and functions that have historically been associated with art: transmitting culture, doing social criticism, providing social cohesion, and contributing to the collective memory.[13] The new technology-based art forms we call "entertainment" were a unique phenomenon that required a different understanding of the relation between art, amusement, and leisure than high culture offered. Going to

---

ton: The Creation of an Organizational Base for High Culture in America," *Media, Culture and Society* 4 (1982): 33-50.

11. Nicholas Wolterstorff, *Art in Action: Toward a Christian Aesthetic* (Grand Rapids: Eerdmans, 1980), p. 27.

12. See Paul Oskar Kristeller, "The Modern System of the Arts," in *Renaissance Thought II: Papers on Humanism and the Arts* (New York: Harper & Row/Harper Torchbooks, 1965), pp. 163-227; Calvin G. Seerveld, *A Turnabout in Aesthetics to Understanding* (Toronto: Wedge Publishing, 1974), pp. 9-10.

13. I am grateful to my colleague Lambert Zuidervaart for help in formulating these functions of art. While the arts have long been recognized as giving symbolic form to life and expressing meaning, they can also provide diversion from cares and concerns, and can satisfy desires unfulfilled in our everyday lives.

dance halls, amusement parks, vaudeville, and movie theaters was not the same as attending the symphony or opera, nor the church revival meeting.

Lacking clear definition, entertainment was defined as that which is not art, usually by virtue of its being a commercial product designed for mass consumption. In 1915, for example, the Supreme Court denied freedom of expression to movies, a decision that had a direct and long-lasting effect on the whole entertainment industry, and was not reversed until 1952. That the industry was controlled by "foreigners," that is, first- and second-generation Jewish immigrants, was not lost on movie reformers; religious antagonisms were clearly behind the crusade against the "menace of the movies."

Without constitutional protection, the film industry was vulnerable to censorship, and the Motion Picture Production Code of 1930 was instituted to control film as a means of cultural transmission and social criticism. By this time, however, the division between high and low or mass culture was reified in American life. The cultural elite now included not only Protestants, but Catholics and Jews; not just the Victorians, but also progressive modernists, who had no devotion to the preservation of Victorian values. Efforts at social control were based on the establishment of an American civil religion. Belief in technological and economic progress, nationalism, a Judeo-Christian morality, and the supposedly self-evident superiority of Western civilization became the foundation for a common American faith and the means of a national cultural consensus. During the 1930s, the phrase "American Dream" came into common usage, and as Susman observed, "Americans then began thinking in terms of patterns of behavior and belief, values and life-styles, symbols and meanings" in reference to an "American way of life."[14]

Industry self-regulation relegated movies, and the other popular culture industries, to a specific role as a provider of harmless or innocent amusement for the entire family. Every movie had to be suitable for viewing by a twelve-year-old. While prior censorship freed the film industry from government regulation, it also prohibited film from maturing and serving the roles for art already

14. See Susman, *Culture as History,* p. 154.

mentioned. As film historian Robert Sklar observed, the code "cut the movies off from many of the most important moral and social themes of the contemporary world."[15] In this regard at least, it is understandable that critics and educators had a difficult time thinking about movies as legitimate art.

*   *   *

There is a long history of religious protest against entertainment. Second-century church father Tertullian condemned the theater as a reflection of the pagan spirit of Rome. John Calvin banned it in Geneva in the sixteenth century; Puritans wrote books condemning Elizabethan drama as an instrument of the Devil. In the American colonies, the House of Representatives of New Hampshire banned an acting company in 1762 on the grounds that the theater had a "peculiar influence on the minds of young people, and greatly endanger[ed] their morals by giving them a taste for intriguing, amusement and pleasure." Theater historian Mendel Kohansky suggested that "the church sees in the theatre a competitor, because the theatre opens vistas to the audience that religion considers its exclusive domain. The power of the actor to lead the audience beyond the limits of everyday experience, to experiences of much great[er] intensity and purity, is a direct threat to organized religion."[16]

The more powerful entertainment became as a force in American life, the greater the fear in the religious community of its potential as an instrument for evil. Many Protestant and Catholic leaders infused the cultural turmoil around the turn of the century with a spiritual dimension. Instead of responding to the entertainment industry as any other aspect of life that is corrupted by sin and in need of transformation, they perceived it as part of a spiritual attack on Christian values and social institutions that imperiled not only the nation, but the kingdom of God and righteous living. In a climate of

15. Robert Sklar, *Movie-Made America: A Cultural History of American Movies* (New York: Random/Vintage Books, 1976), p. 174.
16. Mendel Kohansky, *The Disreputable Profession: The Actor in Society* (Westport, Conn.: Greenwood Press, 1984), pp. 9, 139.

fear, many conservative Protestant groups banned the "amusements," including card playing, dancing, popular music, radio, novel reading, vaudeville, movies, and even the legitimate theater.[17]

The Christian Reformed Church also banned movie and theater attendance. In neo-Calvinist thinking, by virtue of God's "common grace," believers and unbelievers alike are given good gifts to use in service of the cultural mandate, the command to explore and cultivate the possibilities in God's creation. And yet there exists a fundamental and universal spiritual opposition between the dominion of God and that of Satan. This spiritual "antithesis" between good and evil, light and darkness, leaves no aspect of created life untouched. It is a cosmic struggle between "cultural activity in faith and unbelief," Klaas Schilder wrote.[18] These two doctrines, common grace and the antithesis, formed the theological basis of the debate regarding movie attendance, which was one of the most hotly contested issues in the denomination for over half a century.

The confluence of the cultural hierarchy and spiritual antithesis and their sociological associations informed CRC thinking on the matter of the amusements, indicated by the designation "worldly." In that sense, they are good working principles for analysis. Although the rhetoric of CRC leaders often identified high and

---

17. Some evangelicals have completely rejected all culture, regardless of high and low categories, as unspiritual, while others have used popular culture for worship or evangelism. Charles D. Fuller used national radio broadcasts in the 1940s to spread the gospel, and in the 1950s and 1960s Billy Graham employed television and movies for the same purpose. Graham and earlier revivalists all used popular music in their crusades. Beginning in the late 1960s, young evangelicals christianized secular rock music with religious lyrics, and today the contemporary Christian music (CCM) industry is a multimillion-dollar business combining religious worship and evangelism with entertainment. Televangelist Pat Robertson established the Christian Broadcasting Network (CBN), a satellite network designed to beam the Christian gospel around the world. Ironically, while evangelicals today rail against contemporary popular culture and the media as part of an assault on "traditional values," they are at the same time rejecting tradition and the past in praise and worship services, turning to contemporary music and television programming as modes of expression.

18. Klaas Schilder, *Christ and Culture,* trans. G. van Rongen and W. Helder (Winnipeg: Premier, 1977), p. 47.

low culture with righteousness and sin respectively, closer examination reveals a greater complexity to this issue within the ethno-religious community of the Christian Reformed.

Like all immigrant groups, the Dutch Christian Reformed hungered for social respectability and acceptance in American life. They were at once devoted to their religious tradition and producer-oriented values while also seeking to establish themselves in America without imitating its secular practices. Entertainment, and especially the movie industry with its godlike stars and opulent exhibition palaces resembling cathedrals, symbolized both the culture of consumption and a competing religious order. On both counts it threatened to stain the purity of the CRC by homogenizing and nationalizing their ethno-religious community. Further, as a fundamental agent of communication and socialization, the entertainment media challenged the authority and communal control that family and church had over the nurture and enculturation of its members. Nevertheless, what could have developed into an important insight about the emerging structure of modern society was overwhelmed by a pietistic concern with the (im)morality of entertainment.

In a 1928 report entitled "Worldly Amusements in the Light of Scripture," a CRC synodical committee identified three (now famous) "worldly amusements" — gambling, dancing, and the theater/movies. The signficance of this cannot be underestimated. One church historian said, "These three 'don'ts' would play an important role in the history of the denomination, and for several decades were identified by some as the essence of what it meant to be Christian Reformed."[19] The church was actually standing on traditional ground in this matter, for Abraham Kuyper himself banned these same three activities.[20] But within the scope of their

19. Jacob D. Eppinga, *A Century of Grace* (Grand Rapids: LaGrave Avenue Christian Reformed Church, 1987), p. 87.

20. Abraham Kuyper identified the same three in his Princeton Stone Lectures in 1898. "Our fathers perceived excellently well that it was just these three: Dancing, Card-playing, and Theater going, with which the world was madly in love. . . . For this very reason, they recognized in these three the *Rubicon* which no true Calvinist could cross without sacrificing his earnestness to dangerous mirth, and the fear of the Lord to often far from spotless pleasures." Abraham Kuyper, *Lectures on Calvinism* (Grand Rapids: Eerdmans, 1931), pp. 75-76.

wholistic view of cultural engagement, the CRC was in self-contradiction over popular culture.

While the synodical committee acknowledged that theater in and of itself was "not an unclean thing," nevertheless the report stated explicitly that the concern of the committee was "with *the theater* — the theater as it is — not the theater as it might be." On that basis, the committee concluded that "the theater as an institution, taken in its general influence, is on the side of Satan against the Kingdom of Christ." The line of the antithesis was drawn, sequestering the CRC from the movies and other amusements, and, consequently, prohibiting church members from distinguishing redemptive aspects and establishing appropriate Christian participation. As a result, they considered entertainment to be apostate cultural forms not worthy of transformation. Total abstinence was recommended, and they stated further that "it is exceedingly difficult, if not altogether impossible, for us to conceive of a Christian who can conscientiously engage in this kind of work."[21] CRC leaders condemned entertainment as inherently evil, and disallowed any Reformed influence in the popular culture industries. *Banner* editor H. J. Kuiper flailed the movies as "godless," a "moral bubonic plague," a "maelstrom of iniquity," and even the place "where Satan has his throne."[22]

The 1928 synod decision showed the influence of, and strongly resembled, the cultural separatism of American fundamentalism. As James Bratt observed, "Large portions of the Christian Reformed rationale were simple plagiarism of Fundamentalist authors, and the latters' 'legalistic ethics,' nature-grace dualism, and resignation of the world (or certain parts thereof) to the devil — all quite con-

21. The committee saw "no essential difference between the playhouse and the movie theater." "Report of the Committee on Worldly Amusements," *Agenda: Synod of the Christian Reformed Church, 1928,* pp. 31-33, 36.

22. The quoted material here is taken from the following *Banner* articles by H. J. Kuiper: "Sodom and Gomorrah," 12 December 1947, p. 1380; "Moving Pictures," 4 December 1931, p. 1076. As late as 1947, Kuiper called the cinema "one of the most effective inventions of the devil to seduce our covenant-children and drag them into the streets of this modern Sodom and Gomorrah." See "Sodom and Gomorrah," 12 December 1947, p. 1380.

trary to Calvinist norms."[23] This represented a denial of the universality of the spiritual antithesis insofar as this division carved the creation up into aspects worthy of transformation and others to be abandoned to the forces of secularism. There were direct social implications as well. The movies were "morally filthy," Kuiper explained, because "human nature is sinful. Too many movie patrons demand the salacious, the suggestive, the naughty, to make really good movies profitable."[24] The tastes of the unregenerate and the masses were too easily equated.

This was also the case with popular music. Using the scheme of the antithesis, Kuiper wrote: "We believe that there are two kinds of music, radically different — the one inspired by the Spirit of God, the other by demons. The former is truly melodious and harmonious reminding one of heavenly perfection; the later, in its crazy rhythm, its sensual swing, and hideous tunes, reflects the spirit of hell." Kuiper associated musical elements themselves with the spiritual antithesis. He continued: "The fact that the unregenerate may still be able to compose classical music or to enjoy Beethoven and Mendelssohn is truly remarkable. If sin reigned in us unhindered, appreciation of good music would be impossible." Only those among the unregenerate masses, Kuiper implied, could possibly find "pleasure in listening to the baby talk of the boop-a-doop girl, the utter inanity of the verse of 'Mairzy Doats,' or the crooning of Sinatra and his ilk."[25]

In contrast, Kuiper argued, the best among Christians would prefer lectures, sacred concerts, and educational films, exhibiting

23. James D. Bratt, *Dutch Calvinism in Modern America: A History of a Conservative Subculture* (Grand Rapids: Eerdmans, 1984), pp. 116-17.

24. H. J. Kuiper, "The Movie Problem III," *The Banner*, 26 March 1937, p. 293. As early as 1909, one CRC minister wrote that the motion picture apparatus may have been a "wonderful invention" and movies "a valuable production of art, especially for educational purposes," but the film industry catered to public desire for the "spectacular and exciting," producing films designed to "appeal the most to the corrupt taste of the largest portion of the masses." Rather than urge Christians to transform the burgeoning film industry, this minister concluded that "God's name can never be glorified, and His kingdom will never be furthered by co-operating with such institutions of the world." D. De Beer, "Vaudettes," *The Banner*, 30 September 1909, pp. 636-37.

25. H. J. Kuiper, "Foolish Song," Editorial, *The Banner*, 5 May 1944, p. 412.

behavior that showed that CRC people were "distinctive even in their amusements and are developing refined and elegant tastes," he wrote. Once again, this suggests both a desire for social acceptance and an association of most popular culture with the "customs and habits of the unregenerate."[26]

It should be emphasized that the CRC's overriding concern here was with remaining religiously pure. As they applied restrictions to the phenomena around them as a defense against worldliness, the tendency was to reduce spirituality to immorality, and that to sexual impurity. In this respect at least, distinctions between high and low culture did not matter much. "Our amusements, our art, our music, our literature reek with sex filth," Kuiper wrote. "There is no domain where sin has wrought more havoc than in that of the sexual instinct."[27] Even in this regard, however, Kuiper distinguished traditional high art from contemporary modernist forms, associating the later with moral and spiritual deterioration; a practice that resembles that of social and religious conservatives today. "The spirit of sensuality comes to frank expression in many artistic productions," he submitted. "Music must be 'hot,' literature must be 'realistic,' poetry must be impressionistic or cater to the base passions. Modern art — much of it — betrays the gradual sinking of humanity to lower levels of corruption."[28] High art forms were not exempt from religious discernment, but the CRC's application of the antithesis as it equated worldliness and modernism led to a moral and spiritual condemnation of both high and popular expressions of contemporary culture. Instead of critically engaging contemporary culture, the CRC drew a tight circle, in effect cutting themselves off from much of American culture (both high and low).

This theologically informed attitude severely restricted application of the Reformed critique; morality and spirituality became

26. H. J. Kuiper, "Protecting Our Children," *The Banner,* 27 January 1933, p. 77; "Moral Lethargy," *The Banner,* 10 January 1930, p. 28. As early as 1916, a *Banner* writer argued that "habitual attendance at the Movie blunts the intellect, dulls the reasoning power and weakens the emotions and imagination. . . . The Movie is raising a generation of intellectual midgets." J. C. Lobbes, "The Menace of the Movies," *The Banner,* 27 July 1916, p. 468.

27. H. J. Kuiper, "Frankly Sensual," *The Banner,* 26 July 1929, p. 516.

28. H. J. Kuiper, "Foolish Song," Editorial, *The Banner,* 5 May 1944, p. 412.

the primary determinants of the quality and acceptability of art, diminishing aesthetic considerations. Much like evangelical culture today, a lot of sentimental songs and pollyannish fiction passed as Christian hymns and reading material in CRC congregations; pious themes and lyrics substituted for artistic standards. This was perhaps somewhat an embarrassment to the next and more educated generation.

* * *

It is clear from the large number of appeals to Synod, beginning as early as 1932, that CRC members were not content with the church's stance on entertainment. Synod of 1951 was not ready to abandon its long-standing position, but also could not, one committee member said later, "be so unenlightened and so unbiblical as to put a blanket condemnation on one of the most influential and significant of modern art forms" in the twentieth century.[29] Consequently, Synod concluded that movie attendance was not necessarily sinful, although the church would still not condone it. The resolution was ambiguous, if not contradictory, neither condemning nor endorsing the cinema, but making movie attendance a matter of individual conscience.[30]

The interpretation proved portentous. Allowed discriminate attendance, the Christian Reformed flocked to the theaters in 1965 to see *The Sound of Music,* a musical starring Julie Andrews that showed a loving family, bonded together by strong convictions, outwitting the evil Nazis. *The Sound of Music* convinced many, I have discovered, that movies did have potential for service in the kingdom of God. In addition, the growing prevalence of television in CRC homes paved the way for a synodical reevaluation of its position on film.

The following year, a synodical committee examined "film and the film industry not merely as amusements but as a manifestation of culture." Reversing nearly forty years of prohibitions, this com-

29. Henry Stob, "Are Movies Contraband?" *The Reformed Journal,* May-June 1964, p. 5.
30. *Acts of Synod 1951 of the Christian Reformed Church,* p. 65.

mittee concluded that film and television were "legitimate cultural medi[a] to be used by the Christian in the fulfillment of the cultural mandate," and urged the denomination to "engage in a responsible critique of the film arts." The committee suggested that courses be taught at its colleges, reviews published in church periodicals, and that Reformed Calvinists initiate the production of films "bearing the stamp of the regenerate mind and heart."[31]

Calvin entered a new era in its history after World War II and inaugurated a curricular reform that was completed in 1968 and published as *Christian Liberal Arts Education (CLAE)*. Calvin professors, with doctorates from Harvard and Yale now, applied the Reformed critique to every discipline, including study of the arts and literature. The new disciplinary model rejected the "classicist" approach in part because its emphasis on "understanding and judging culture, not on contributing to it," was too passive for neo-Calvinists who were "convinced that the great and continuing task of the Christian community on earth is to *build* a culture."[32] In practical design, however, the curriculum privileged the classical disciplines, resulting unfortunately in a dismissal of contemporary popular culture. English professor Henry Zylstra, for example, broke new ground and pushed the envelope in the CRC community when he argued for the value of reading novels because they can "instruct while they entertain." But by literature, Zylstra meant the canon of literary classics and not popular fiction, which was "mere entertainment," "canned opiate or tonic for frightened or bored people," he wrote.[33] Likewise, in the face of Synod's declaration against theater, Calvin could introduce "play acting" (and

31. *The Church and the Film Arts*, Henry C. Van Deelen, chairman (Grand Rapids: Christian Reformed Publishing House, 1967), pp. 5, 33, 38.

32. *Christian Liberal Arts Education: Report of the Calvin College Curriculum Study Committee* (Grand Rapids: Calvin College and Eerdmans, 1970), p. 46. Also to avoid the pragmatic trend toward vocational specialization that was in vogue at the time, the college adopted a "disciplinary" model requiring a large number of general core requirements to ensure the development of a Reformed worldview, while also allowing students to concentrate in a specific area by selecting a major requiring comparatively fewer courses.

33. Henry Zylstra, *Testament of Vision* (Grand Rapids: Eerdmans, 1958, 1961), pp. 46, 50-51.

not without some restrictions) in the 1950s, but movies remained a cultural taboo.

As this suggests, the Reformed "barometer for gauging the spiritual weather" was identified as high culture.[34] In this scheme, high culture was perceived as the critical arena in which religious and cultural forces battled, shaping and reflecting the *Zeitgeist*. Regarding the arts, the architects of the *CLAE* document concluded: "Not only does a study of the arts enhance the joy and delight which is to be found in the arts and which is so valuable a part of the full Christian life; also, it engages us with some of the richest, clearest, and most vivid manifestations of human religious commitment." Literature, moreover, deserved a special place in the curriculum because of its "greater explicitness" "of ideas and convictions" than the other arts, and because "literature written in English is the most accessible to the majority of our students and the most formative of our own culture."[35] In other words, it was in high culture that the spirit of an age or a people was best expressed and determined, reaching the masses via a trickling-down effect.

To a large extent, Calvin, like other Christian liberal arts colleges, became a repository of traditional high culture, to the exclusion, at least from the formal curriculum, of popular culture. In one sense, this is not surprising; popular culture, gender, and ethnic studies did not begin to make inroads into academia until the late 1960s and early 1970s. Even so, the reification of high and low culture in the academy and decades of denominational prohibitions had created a blindspot; it is debatable whether literature, and high culture for that matter, played such a prominent role in the lives of most young people at the time. Even if this notion were correct, it is certainly no longer true, even among CRC youth. Almost immediately after Synod's legitimation of the cinema, it became clear that young people in the CRC, like most young evangelicals, displayed greater participation in the youth subculture than in one that was an expression of shared religious values.[36]

34. This quote is taken from ibid., pp. 5-6.
35. *Christian Liberal Arts Education*, p. 82.
36. "Report 27: Committee on Youth and Young-Adult Ministry," *Agenda for Synod 1991*, pp. 346-47, 356. The results of this survey revealed that media

In the decades after World War II, an age-segregated youth culture emerged across class, racial, and ethnic lines. During the same period, in a series of decisions beginning in 1952, the U.S. Supreme Court extended First Amendment rights to film and differentiated obscenity standards for adults and minors. These decisions led to the dissolution of the various production codes in the popular art industries, and coincided with a significant shift in audience, from a general family market to a specific segment, the under-thirty demographic. The entertainment industries began asserting their artistic freedom just as popular culture became the province of the young (and the CRC permitted movie attendance). As adolescents became the primary consumers of popular culture, the industries shifted their output from family-oriented products to rock music and movies like *Bonnie and Clyde, The Graduate,* and *Easy Rider,* which were designed to appeal to this new "teenage" social group in America.[37]

Following Synod's legitimation of film and television, the Calvin Film Council was established to select movies for viewing on campus. The cinema remained a Christian Reformed symbol for worldliness, but among the CRC's postwar generation the contemporary media and popular culture represented the voice of youth, and in the late 1960s, radical youth. Controversies erupted between students and administrators over which films could be shown, one of the most famous being *A Clockwork Orange,* and, more recently, *The Last Temptation of Christ* (scripted by Calvin alumnus Paul Schrader).

*   *   *

The role of the popular arts, as they have been defined as low culture and by the interests of commercialism, has contributed to industry abuses of its artistic freedom, disregard for roles it serves other than appeasing corporate investors, and the exploitation of markets. These are good reasons for criticism, along with the industry's lack

---

usage among young people in the CRC is consistent with a national sampling of the same age group. For comparison, see *America's Youth: 1977-1988,* ed. Robert Bezilla (Princeton, N.J.: Gallup Organization, 1988).

37. See Quentin J. Schultze et al., *Dancing in the Dark: Youth, Popular Culture and the Electronic Media* (Grand Rapids: Eerdmans, 1991).

of inhibition, especially the liberal use of profanity and visceral sexual and violent imagery that can turn a cinematic experience into a roller-coaster ride. When combined with cultural elitism and spiritual denigration, the industry's seemingly iconoclastic portrayals can make it difficult for some even to consider the possibility of a transforming presence in Hollywood. These critics, however, have confused the issue by identifying the potentials of the popular arts for service of God and neighbor with the forces of secularism as they have been at work in the culture industries.

This has contributed to a refusal on the part of some to acknowledge the importance of popular culture, an attitude that involves a willful blindness and even hypocrisy, especially for neo-Calvinists. Popular art forms are a significant part of the artistic fabric of our society, and entertainment has become an important social institution centering on human needs for both leisure and artistic interpretations of our lives and times. The hallmark of a Reformed critical approach has been uncovering and disentangling the dominant religious and cultural forces at work in our lives and society. And the products and practices associated with popular culture represent a powerful and effectual expression of the spirit of our age. Popular culture influences how people think about themselves, their relation to others, and their place in society. The entertainment media in particular inform, explore controversial moral and social issues, help people navigate through the complexity of our rapidly changing world, and offer visions of life.

We should study popular culture today for the same reasons Zylstra promoted the reading of novels in the 1950s. Popular music, movies, television, and other aspects of popular culture "instruct while they entertain," and are a vital means to uncover the spiritual forces at work in our world, and especially in the youth culture, where popular culture continues to play a crucial developmental role.[38] Also, the study of popular culture seems particularly signifi-

---

38. Even the late Allan Bloom, an elitist and champion of classicism, observed that the producers of entertainment "have the strongest motives for finding out the appetites of the young — so they are useful guides into the labyrinths of the spirit of the times." *The Closing of the American Mind* (New York: Simon and Schuster, 1987), p. 19.

cant in light of the church's history of cultural involvement. Religious convictions seem inevitably to become entangled with the social and cultural forces that are supposed to be the objects of reform. For some, this has tarnished the transformational model — if not the ideal, at least the historical practice — and has raised important questions about the relation between worldview (i.e., the "Christian mind") and culture. The historical record and experience suggests a more reciprocal relation perhaps than the Reformed tradition has maintained, and one requiring constant critical discernment of contemporary culture.[39]

Furthermore, technological advance promises not only the continued viability of electronic-based popular art, but its expansion with new formats and delivery systems that will intensify the entertainment experience, while increasing access and availability. Three major conclusions from social science research on the impact of the media point to a "visual" or media literacy component in the curriculum as a viable course of action for those interested in reform. First, the impact of the media is not homogenous, but specific to individuals and mediated by a large number of variables including age, personal temperament and viewing skills, gender, ethnicity, family and neighborhood, education, community standards, political perspective, and social and economic status. Second, the media are more influential when other social institutions are weak. Finally, research on the effects of television viewing has identified preadolescent childhood as the critical period of exposure to the entertainment media. This suggests that interventions should begin in the home and elementary schools.[40] It follows from these conclusions that an important avenue for reform is to influence the audience through involvement at the institutional level.

39. See Paul A. Marshall, Sander Griffioen, and Richard J. Mouw, eds., *Stained Glass: Worldviews and Social Science* (Latham: University Press of America, 1989). This also undermines the pedagogical viability of a Reformed application of the classicist argument that introducing students to the right ideas or a canon of classics is sufficient to equip them to critically engage the forces of secularism in their contemporary setting and work toward reformation.

40. See Brandon S. Centerwall, "Television and Violence: The Scale of the Problem and Where to Go from Here," *JAMA* 267 (10 June 1992): 3059-63.

Unfortunately, educational institutions are out of sync with the most "popular" and perhaps most influential cultural forms and social practices today, as well as the sensibilities of current generations. That we do not include popular culture in the formal curriculum implies that we can get along without theorizing about it, or paying it much serious critical attention. Outside the classroom, however, students are such avid consumers of popular culture that the idea that young people must be protected from the culture industries is no longer realistic, let alone a viable assumption to use in constructing strategies for reform. This suggests the need for reform in our social arrangement in order to bring popular culture into the sphere of public discourse, instead of leaving it to the forces of the marketplace.

The inclusion of popular culture in the curriculum does not mean that students play with Barbie dolls and watch MTV or reruns of *Beavis and Butthead* all day. Most students already have plenty of exposure to popular culture, but do not think critically enough about it. Rather, the purpose is to bring popular culture into our formal arena for analysis so that people learn to critically engage popular culture and the media in association with their experience with other institutions that help shape their identities, basic convictions, and perspectives on life. This is not an easy task, because people do not experience popular culture in the abstract; it is woven into the fabric of life. Popular culture studies, then, cannot simply be modeled after the canonized approach in traditional literature, music, or art appreciation courses, but requires a different pedagogy in part because of its existential immediacy.

There are at least four general aspects to popular culture studies and a visual literacy component in the curriculum. Briefly, popular culture has to be considered seriously in the study of the humanities as part of the terrain of social, cultural, historical, political, and religious life. Second, popular culture "texts" (i.e., cultural products) can be used in the study of other subjects. Examining treatment of a historical event like Vietnam, for example, in the news media, as well as in movies, television programming, comic books, and popular fiction, can help students to understand the valuable contribution the arts and media make to our collective memory, how they can provide social unity, while also exploring the ways our culture is transmitted and social criticism is done. Third, addressing visual literacy entails the design of specific courses to help students to understand both *how* the media communicate (e.g., filmic conventions) and *what* is communicated (beliefs, values, moral, religious, and ideological perspectives). Students need to think critically about these as well as the cult of hyperbole, sensation, consumption, and mass identification that the culture industries propagate. Finally, teaching about the media necessarily involves emerging technologies. Just as literary studies consist of both textual analysis and composition, so the study of visual communication requires an understanding of the methods of production and decision making in the construction of media images.

Rethinking our ideas about high and popular culture can work to create a better place for the traditional arts in everyday life, while also granting popular culture forms their legitimate role. But there are even broader implications for this kind of analysis as it relates to issues of justice and curricular matters.

African-American culture, for example, has often been treated as somehow primitive or inferior, based on the standards and institutional structure of Anglo-American high culture. But the black church is one of the most dynamic illustrations of the integration of faith and culture in the twentieth century. Bonded together not only by a history of oppression but also by their racial and religious identity, African-Americans fashioned a distinct cultural tradition rooted in the Christian faith, not only in sermons and worship but in social life, politics, and the arts. Though African-Americans represent only 13 percent of the population, "they dominate the nation's popular culture: its music, its dance, its talk, its sports, its youths' fashion; and they are a powerful force in its popular and elite literature," one scholar recently observed. "A black music, jazz, is the nation's classical voice, defining, audibly, its entire civilizational style."[41] Black musicians and musi-

41. Orlando Patterson, "The Paradox of Integration," *The New Republic,* 6 November 1995, p. 24. Categorical cultural distinctions along gender lines have also made an impact on the curriculum. The description of mass culture as feminine beginning in the 1920s, e.g., worked to designate women's culture as popular and therefore justify its exclusion from institutions of high culture. See Maltby, *Passing Parade,* p. 13.

cal styles were the impetus for every vital new movement in American popular music, representing America's greatest contributions to the world of music. The black church was the central institution in the modern Civil Rights movement; the Black Power movement's assertion that racism (i.e., sin) is both personal and institutional resonates with Reformed thinking. Certainly there is something of the "best that has been thought and said" in African-American life for Reformed Christians to learn about cultural transformation and the struggle with secularization.

*   *   *

We are experiencing a profound shift today in the historical conditions that maintained the cultural consensus reached during the Depression and World War II; the breakup of that consensus has brought a return of cultural strife.[42] Urbanization and industrialization have given way to suburbanization and the age of information and communication. Long-term economic growth has been interrupted by periods of recession and unemployment; our national economy and policy are increasingly shaped by global concerns and competition. Social institutions are under strain trying to keep pace with major changes in work and society brought about by economic dislocation and technological advance.

Current immigration trends are comparable with those at the beginning of this century. The assimilationist "melting pot," however, has been replaced with an emphasis on maintaining a distinct subcultural identity, while still being an American; the integration goals of the 1950s and 1960s have shifted to the creation of a wholly multicultural society. This in turn has given rise to new cultural identities and political factions, mirrored in the intellectual force of postmodernism with its emphasis on the validity of diverse perspectives based on race, gender, sexuality, nationality, ethnicity, and, to a lesser extent perhaps, religion.

As a result of these social and intellectual developments, the conceptual and social borders between high and low culture are

42. See Godfrey Hodgson, *America in Our Time* (New York: Doubleday, 1976).

dissolving, within both intellectual circles and the culture industries. Scholars have come to recognize that high and popular culture have much in common as human social practices, and have begun to trace their mutual influence. "The redefinition of popular culture studies has made problematic earlier views of mass culture as degraded and elite culture as elevating," the editors of a recent volume explained. "Instead, the new studies recognize the power of the ordinary, accept the commonplace as a legitimate object of inquiry, hammer away at the often arbitrary and ideological distinctions between popular, mass, and elite culture, and ask serious questions about the role of popular culture in political and social life."[43]

The erosion of the barriers between high and low culture, however, challenges the Anglo-American hegemony. At issue in today's culture wars, like those at the beginning of the century, is control over "the" national culture and the use of established institutions to maintain cultural consensus or to express diversity. The current debate is extremely politicized, embroiled in battles between political parties and ideologies of the left and right, over freedom of expression for new ideas and perspectives against maintaining the authority of traditional values.

According to James Davison Hunter's configuration of today's conflict, evangelicalism has aligned itself with the orthodox or conservative side.[44] Armed with its premillennial eschatology that has the country going to hell, evangelicalism has equated the culture and values of the Anglo-American tradition with moral righteousness and the Truth (with a capital T), as though a neo-Victorian model can repair the cultural cleavages in the divided and perplexed society it helped to create, and reinvent a cultural consensus. Opposing cultural pluralism as an assault on the core values of Western civilization, evangelical leaders have joined social conservatives in their condemnation of contemporary art and entertainment as cul-

43. Chandra Mukerji and Michael Schudson, eds., *Rethinking Popular Culture: Contemporary Perspectives in Cultural Studies* (Berkeley: University of California Press, 1991), p. 2.
44. James Davison Hunter, *Culture Wars: The Struggle to Define America* (New York: Basic Books, 1991).

tural decadence.[45] Conservative media critics advocate a nostalgic return to the mythological consensus of the Studio Era (1930-1950), "the Golden Age of Motion Pictures when Mr. Smith went to Washington and it was a wonderful life," as one critic put it.[46]

On the other side, progressives generally view popular culture as an expression of democratic pluralism, representing, both symbolically and practically, new ideas and perspectives, as well as the culture of marginal and less powerful groups.[47] The pluralist view, however, still has to contend with the problem of order and the difficulty of maintaining cultural consensus within society. And in its more extreme versions, the progressive response to a history of hegemony has tended to overemphasize the relativity of culture, even denying critique of one culture based on the moral or cultural perspective of others.

Today's cultural tumult creates a particular challenge as Calvin tries to navigate a Reformed course through the landscape of premillennialism and postmodernism, that is, evangelicalism's efforts to establish its own cultural hegemony, and a postmodern pluralism that either abandons the possibility of truth or pretends that all

45. Bloom, e.g., described culture in Arnoldian terms as "something high, profound, respectable — a thing before which we bow," and made absolute qualitative distinctions between high and low culture, seeing "no relation between popular culture and high culture," and lamenting that "the former is all that is now influential on our scene." Bloom proposed that young people take off their Walkmans and listen instead to the Greek and European savants of Western civilization. *Closing of the American Mind*, pp. 185, 187, 322, 69, 75.

46. Ted Baehr, quoted in Joe Maxwell, "The New Hollywood Watchdogs," *Christianity Today*, 27 April 1992, p. 39. See also Michael Medved, *Hollywood Vs. America: Popular Culture and the War on Traditional Values* (New York: Harper-Collins/Zondervan, 1992). Constitutional issues regarding free speech make such an appeal unrealistic, as the consensus exhibited by movies during the Studio Era depended on the prior censorship of the Motion Picture Production Code.

47. Progressives propose a multicultural curriculum that does not focus exclusively on the dominant Anglo-American tradition, but includes works by women, African-Americans, Native Americans, Asian-Americans, Latinos, gays, and others. See, e.g., Stanley Aronowitz, *Roll Over Beethoven: The Return of Cultural Strife* (Hanover: Wesleyan University Press, 1993); Henry A. Giroux and Roger I. Simon et al., *Popular Culture, Schooling, and Everyday Life* (Westport, Conn.: Bergin & Garvey Publishers, 1989).

cultures more or less equally lead to truth.[48] A Reformed understanding of culture, however, as the God-given mandate to explore and cultivate the possibilities woven into the creation, allows for cultural pluralism, while affirming the existence of a world ordered by God. The directive to be "in the world but not of it" implies that Christians ought to be both cultural formers and reformers, measuring cultural development against the principles of love, truth, justice, and stewardship. A Reformed perspective, then, is solid ground amid the centrifugal tendencies in our postmodern world. It allows for analysis of former and contemporary cultural endeavors as representing the myriad ways that humans have responded to the cultural mandate, resulting in both blessing and curse.

In a creative tension with its past, Calvin seeks to move forward with a distinctly Reformed approach amid today's cultural strife. The college has already made an institutional commitment to becoming "a genuinely multicultural Christian academic community" as "a credible witness to the culturally diverse character of the Kingdom of God." There is an effort to internationalize the curriculum so that "Calvin graduates will know and appreciate cultures other than those dominant in North America and Western Europe."[49] Gender and popular culture studies have made some inroads into the curriculum. An introductory film course, one in popular music, and another in television criticism were gradually instituted at Calvin beginning in the 1970s. Recently, Film Studies was established as a concentration in Communication Arts and Sciences.

Scholarship and curriculum should represent all that the institution deems important about knowledge, culture, and society, remembering that if students are to be transformers of culture, they must be able to confront the world as it exists to envision possibilities for its betterment. To that end, today's students should be given

48. I am paraphrasing, in a somewhat different context, Rodney Clapp, "Calling the Religious Right to Its Better Self," *Perspectives,* April 1994, p. 13.

49. "Comprehensive Plan for Integrating North American Ethnic Minority Persons and Their Interests into Every Facet of Calvin's Institutional Life," December 1985.

the critical skills to access any cultural text, literature, and audio-visual media. If such an endeavor were to include the European symphony and African-American blues, Shakespeare and Spielberg, Dickens and *N.Y.P.D. Blue,* Henry James and Oprah Winfrey, hymnody and contemporary Christian music — now that would be entertaining . . . and instructive. Appreciating how these cultural forms and practices coexist, relate to, and influence each other, and understanding the place of minority perspectives in the course of history and study of the contemporary world can serve as an integrating influence in our postmodern society. Seeing creation, culture, and society as a whole and yet complex interacting environment is a sign of a Reformed vision; granting religious pluralism and cultural diversity a capacity based on the belief in the centrality of religion to human existence in a fallen world.

In the ongoing historical struggle between the commitments of Christianity and the forces of secularism, Calvin has not only maintained its purpose, distinctive religious identity, and intellectual tradition, but has distinguished itself as a Christian liberal arts college in the Reformed tradition. Though conservative when it comes to change ("If it ain't broke, why fix it?"), the institution has critically engaged pressing issues, in part by asserting the Reformed conviction that although a culture has deep roots in the past, it is a living, dynamic process rather than a static legacy. Culture and society are unfinished entities, living traditions and conditions that change as we contribute to them.

Should the Work of Our Hands Have Standing in the Christian College?

Nicholas P. Wolterstorff

I propose on this occasion reversing the customary order of academic lectures by leading off with my conclusion. Such dramatic tension as there may be on this occasion will have to come from your not knowing how I am going to get to where I am going rather than from your not knowing where I am going. But first, a true story.

It must be about fifteen years ago now, when I was still teaching at Calvin College, that I received a call from the personnel manager at the Herman Miller Corporation asking whether I would be willing to come over to their head offices in Zeeland, Michigan, to spend a day as consultant. Now I can assure you, in case you have ever wondered, that philosophers are not often asked to serve as consultants. It is, admittedly, not entirely unheard of. A few years back an unemployed philosopher in Amsterdam opened a philosophical consulting service on the premise that many of the problems people experience in their lives are best addressed not by psychological, vocational, or pastoral counseling, but by philosophical counseling. They have logical problems, ontological problems, axiological problems, epistemological problems, and so forth. I understand he has been a considerable success. But that is the Dutch for you! All in all, it is a rare experience for a philosopher to be asked to serve as counselor or consultant.

I accepted, partly because I was intrigued, and partly — let me be candid — because the fee offered made me understand instantly why those who can consult do consult. It turned out that there were five of us consultants, from around the country: a journalist, a lawyer, a physician who worked for NASA, a free-lance furniture designer, and myself, a philosopher. We met with five or six of the head people at Herman Miller, including Max De Pree, who was then chief executive officer of the company. Max led off the discussion by saying that about twice a year he and some of his chief executives took a day out from their regular work to stand back and reflect with a small group of people on what they were doing at Herman Miller. It had been their experience at the company, he said, that a reflective retreat of this sort was very important for keeping the big picture in mind. Max said that he had written down ten questions that he would like us to discuss. He did not care in what order we discussed them, nor even whether we actually got around to discussing all of them. But these ten were on his mind. We, the consultants, were not to concern ourselves with how our discussion might be useful to the company; we were to let the discussion flow. The people from the company would decide what to do with what was said.

Let me mention three of the questions De Pree posed to us; they will give the flavor of the whole. What is the purpose of business? he asked. Some of his young executives were saying that the purpose of business is to make money. He himself did not believe that. But he would like us to discuss it. Second, is there a moral imperative to good design? Ever since the thirties, the Herman Miller Company had been committed to good and innovative design. Should that commitment to good design continue, on the ground that good design is a moral imperative, or is good design a dispensable option? And third, is growth compatible with intimacy? The company had always striven for intimacy among its employees. Its rapid growth in recent years, and the pressure of its stockholders for even more growth, was forcing it to ask whether growth is compatible with intimacy.

The breadth and depth of the questions took me completely aback. I, as a philosopher, had expected to be like a fish out of water for a day. This was not only water but my water. These were philosophical questions. I have no memory of what I said. I cannot believe that it proved of much use to the Herman Miller Company, since the issues Max posed were not ones that I had then thought much about. But I remember enjoying the day enormously. I think back to it often. In a number of ways it proved a watershed for me — for example, in my thinking about Christian higher education.

Let me explain. Notice what took place on that day. We were not asked to advise Herman Miller on one or another technological or bureaucratic problem facing it. Nor were we asked to help Herman Miller think through some moral quandary in which it found itself. Truth is, we were not asked to think specifically about Herman Miller at all; the Herman Miller Company was more illustration than topic. We were asked to stand back and think about one of the major social formations in contemporary society, namely, business. We were asked to reflect on the purpose of business and on the imperatives that hold for it. In a word, we were asked to engage in normative reflection on business. Our reflection was meant to aid the normative discrimination of those who operated Herman Miller — to aid them in discriminating between that to which they ought to say Yes and that to which they ought to say No.

Now for my proposal. The Christian college and university should be a place where the Christian community does its thinking about the major social formations of contemporary society — its normative and strategic thinking. It would be acceptable to call the thinking in question critical thinking. That is, the Christian college and university should be a place where the Christian community does its critical thinking about the major social formations of contemporary society — provided critical thinking is not thought of as just negative thinking, and provided it is thought of as going beyond mere evaluation. For the thinking I propose about our contemporary social formations will be neither purely negative nor purely positive. It will neither laud business to the skies nor condemn it to Sheol; it will neither praise American politics unstintingly nor criticize it unrelievedly. It will exhibit and cultivate normative discrimination. And it will go on to ask how what is good can be preserved, and what is wrong, changed. In saying this, I understand myself to be expressing the classic Calvinist attitude toward social formations and institutions: the Christian pronounces not just a Yes on such formations nor just a No, but a discriminating Yes and No. Critical appreciation, appreciative criticism. And that done, the Christian then struggles to act redemptively.

In being a place where the Christian community does its normative and strategic thinking about the major social formations of our society, the Christian college that I envisage will be more than just a liberal arts college; it will, however, be at least that. Since I suspect that this one-sentence disclaimer will not be sufficient to forestall the suspicion that I have come to bury the liberal arts, let me begin by praising them.

To do so, I must explain briefly what I take the liberal arts to be; for there is no consensus on the matter. Everyone agrees that a program of liberal arts education is aimed at something other than training a person for some particular occupational role. It would, of course, be surprising and disappointing if one's liberal arts education had no positive benefits whatsoever for what one does in the occupation in which eventually one finds oneself; but there is no occupational role for which it is the training program. It may well be that when a student is offered curricular options within a program of liberal arts education, she will make her selections with an eye on what will prove most useful for the occupation to which she aspires; she may, thus, follow a pre-law program, or pre-medical, or pre-seminary. But the courses specified in, say, a pre-law program will not themselves be structured as training for lawyers.

The disagreements arise when we move beyond the negative, of what a liberal arts education is not, to say positively what it is. On what it is not, there is consensus; on what it is, there is not. Two major understandings have been in conflict ever since the days of the Renaissance. The older of the two understandings, prominent already in the Middle Ages, is that the aim of liberal arts education is to induct the student into those social practices of discovery that are the academic disciplines and to acquaint the student with their achievements. Philosophy is such a practice of discovery, stretching in this case from the classical Greeks on into our own day; and to us it is abundantly evident, as it was not yet to the ancients and medievals, that philosophy is like social practices in general, not only in that it alters across time in its goals, methods, and criteria for excellence, but in that it is the arena of disputes over its proper goals, methods, and criteria for excellence. Philosophy is internally contested. Sociology, a much more recent practice of discovery, has likewise proved, even in its short history, to be the locus not only of change but of internal contests concerning its proper goals, methods, and criteria for excellence. One understanding of liberal arts education, then, is that it aims at inducting students, some more thoroughly, others less thoroughly, into these changing and internally contested social practices of discovery, and to acquaint them with the achievements of these practices.

Among the so-called humanists of the Renaissance a quite different understanding of education emerged that also has claim to being called "liberal arts education." A point insistently made by anthropologists in our century, but known already from time immemorial, is that, as compared to the rest of the animals, we human beings are radically underdetermined by our biological and physiological makeup. If we are to function at all, not to mention flourish, we have to be cultured — or, better, enculturated. We have to acquire habits of acting, ways of interpreting experience and reality, commitments and beliefs, ways of feeling, and so forth. But since there is no such thing as human culture in general, one cannot be enculturated just into human culture but only into some highly specific form thereof: into twentieth-century American culture, into twelfth-century Byzantine culture, into eighteenth-century Sioux culture, and so forth. And even these descriptions do no more than pick out general patterns of enculturation, rather than identify the cultural formation of particular human beings.

The culture of most human beings is very much a local affair — local as to both time and space. But the fact that we human beings express our enculturation in artifacts, and that a good many of these artifacts endure, makes it possible for one's enculturation to expand beyond the local and parochial. It makes it possible for one's cultural formation to be enlarged by one's incorporation of interpretations and beliefs of those at a distance, and makes it possible for one then to feel, act, and commit oneself in ways appropriate to this expanded enculturation. Liberal arts education, on this alternative understanding, is an educational program that "liberates" one from parochiality in one's cultural formation by opening up before one that vast range of alternative and expanded possibilities.

To my mind, this understanding of liberal arts education has never been better expressed than it was by the contemporary English philosopher Michael Oakeshott, in two eloquent essays, "A Place of Learning" and "Education: The Engagement and Its Frustration."[1] Oakeshott's rhetorical strategy is to argue that true education just is liberal arts education, and that true schools and universities just are places where education, thus understood, takes place. "School," he says, means

> detachment from the immediate, local world of the learner, its current concerns and the directions it gives to his attention, for this (and not "leisure" or "play") is the proper meaning of the word *schole*. "School" is a place apart in which the heir may encounter his moral and intellectual inheritance, not in the terms in which it is being used in the current engagements and occupations of the world outside (where much of it is forgotten, neglected, obscured, vulgarized or abridged, and where it appears only in scraps and as investments in immediate enterprises) but as an estate, entire, unqualified and unencumbered. "School" is an emancipation achieved in a continuous redirection of attention. Here, the learner is animated, not by the inclinations he brings with him, but by intimations of excellence and aspirations he has never yet dreamed of; here he may encounter, not answers to the "loaded" questions of "life," but questions which have never before occurred to him; here he may acquire new "interests" and pursue them uncorrupted by the need for immediate results; here he may learn to seek satisfactions he had never yet imagined or wished for.[2]

I observed that two understandings of liberal arts education — call them respectively the disciplinary and the classicist — have been in competition with each other ever since the Renaissance,

1. Collected along with other essays by Oakeshott on education in *The Voice of Liberal Learning: Michael Oakeshott,* ed. T. Fuller (New Haven: Yale University Press, 1989).
2. Oakeshott, "Education: The Engagement and Its Frustration," ibid., p. 69.

when the so-called humanists attacked the sterility of "the schools" and espoused the classicist understanding as their alternative to the regnant disciplinary understanding. The disciplinary understanding gained new vitality in the Enlightenment from the excitement stirred up by the new science; later, with the emergence of the Romantic concept of Bildung, classicism once again came forth from the shadows. And so the debate continues, back and forth.

The two have always been in competition here at Calvin College as well. Harry Jellema was the great exponent in our midst of the classicist understanding; the 1964 report of the curriculum revision committee, *Christian Liberal Arts Education,* espoused the disciplinary understanding. Neither has ever ousted the other; and now, thirty years after our curricular debates of the 1960s, I am inclined to say that that is probably all to the good! It is true that indecisive debate over the matter does not make for coherence in educational philosophy; but sometimes it is good for institutions to maintain a bit of internal tension.

What must be added is that we at Calvin College have always given a unique and important "twist" to both the disciplinary and classicist understandings. Though the similarity of thought between Michael Oakeshott and Harry Jellema is striking, there remains nonetheless an absolutely fundamental difference. We at Calvin College have always insisted that one cannot engage in liberal arts education, on whichever understanding, in religiously neutral fashion. And if we had believed it could be done, we would not have wanted to do it. Liberal arts education has always been for us an exercise of Christian learning. Christian learning has been our fundamental commitment.

We have articulated for ourselves a number of reasons for engaging in Christian learning. We have said that Christian integrity requires it: If liberal arts education is not and cannot be a religiously neutral enterprise, then our calling is to struggle toward elimination of all double-mindedness, and with singleness of heart to be faithful to God in Jesus Christ in our educational endeavors. We have also said that the vitality of the Christian community requires that there be Christian learning, so as to give content to the community's voice and direction to its action. For a long time, however, I have felt in my bones that neither of these reasons — important though they be — articulates the motivation for Christian learning that is deepest in this community. I can remember yet the excitement I felt when I came as a freshman to Calvin College and was first introduced to Christian learning as here practiced. Young as I was, I felt that I had already seen the rest of my life: I was to be a Christian scholar, like unto those masters who were my teachers. But I do not think what gripped me was either of the two reasons I have cited.

Let me try to articulate what I think it was. I very much like the formulation that Brian Gerrish, theologian at the University of Chicago, gives of the heart of John Calvin's theology. Let me put his thought in my own words: To be human is to be that place in creation where God's goodness is meant to find its answer in gratitude. I think what has always inspired my own engagement in Christian learning — inspiration picked up from my teachers here and reinforced by my colleagues — is the conviction that Christian learning is an act of gratitude to God. Not the only act of gratitude, obviously; and not an act to be performed by every Christian. It is one of the community's acts of gratitude to God. It is extremely important for one purpose and another. But more fundamental than its importance for this and for that is the fact that it is an act of gratitude.

Most of you will know that the Greek word for thanksgiving is *eucharistia*. I think what I imbibed from my teachers and believed all these years, but, strangely, have not until recently been able to articulate, is that learning is a eucharistic act. Though I said, and we all said, that Christian learning is a matter of duty, of obligation — that we ought to be doing it — in my own case it never felt like an obligation lying on my shoulders. It did not feel like something I ought to do. It felt like something I wanted to do — something it was a delight to do, something it was a privilege to do. And not just because it answered to some need in my psyche, but because it had to do with my relation to God. I think that all these years I have been engaging in Christian learning as a eucharistic act. I have never felt the urge to marshall my learning in defense of the faith — though when called to defend it, I will gladly do so. Rather, I have felt that God has invited me to use my learning to become enculturated more deeply into the vast and wonderful legacy of Christian culture: Anselm and Barth, Duccio and Rouault, Donne and Eliot, Perotin and Messiaen, Chartres and Ronchamp. And then, thus enculturated, to advance the exploration of the world of creation and culture in the manner of a scholar. To do so as a Christian; how else was I to do it? Invitation more than duty. It was as if I had asked God: What shall I do in response to your grace? And as if God had said: I invite you to be a scholar.

At the same time that it was for me a eucharistic act, it was an eirenic, or, perhaps better, a shalomic act. I am thinking here of the Old Testament understanding of *shalom* — the word being translated in the New Testament with the Greek word *eirene,* and in our English Bibles as "peace," but much better translated, I think, as "flourishing." I have always believed that learning, faithful learning, contributes to our human flourishing. No doubt it is of use for the alteration of world, society, and self. For me, though, what has always been more important is that it makes the glories of human culture available to us, helps us to interpret what is baffling in our world, provides answers to our questions, suggests new questions. Christian learning is both a eucharistic act and, when properly done, an eirenic, or shalomic, act. Motivated by thanksgiving and charity, upon opening up before us some of "the depth of the riches and wisdom and knowledge of God" (Rom. 11:33, 36), it culminates in praise.

Having now praised Christian liberal arts education, let me go on to observe that within the Reformed ethos of Christianity there is a component that will make the person imbued with this ethos feel uneasy with the tradition of liberal arts education. The Reformed Christian will feel uneasy with the pretensions to neutrality so characteristic of the tradition; but that is a point already made. What I have my eye on now is the elitism so characteristic of the tradition; the person imbued with the ethos of Reformed Christianity will feel uneasy with the claims to superiority made on behalf of engaging in the liberal arts.

In liberal arts education one cultivates the mind — using "mind" here in a sense close to that of the German word *Geist.* And from Plato and Aristotle onward the conviction has never lacked for enthusiastic supporters that the fundamental reason for engaging in the liberal arts, when and where that is possible, is that the life of the mind is the highest form of life available to a human being. Those who espoused the disciplinary understanding of liberal education have said, typically, that contemplative thinking is the noblest of all human activities. Those who espoused the classicist understanding have said, typically, that to expand the scope of one's enculturation by appropriating the culture of those distant in time and space is to become more fully human.[3] Either way, the life of the mind is the highest form of human life.

Plato and Aristotle differed in their assessment of civic life, this to be distinguished both from the life of the mind and from ordinary life. Plato saw in the life of the citizen nothing but instrumental worth; Aristotle saw it as having inherent worth. Though inferior to the life of the mind, it is, said Aristotle, an indispensable component in the good life as a whole. In their assessment of ordinary life, however, Plato and Aristotle were in full agreement: its worth is purely instrumental. Neither the life of the mind nor the life of the citizen is possible without ordinary life. But a life that consists entirely of ordinary life, a life that includes no life of the mind and no civic life, is not a good life. And a society in which everybody's life consists entirely of ordinary life is not even a true state, or polis, says Aristotle. For "the end of the state is not mere life; it is, rather, a good quality of life. [If mere life were the end], there might be a state of slaves, or even a state of animals; but in the world as we know it any such state is impossible, because slaves and animals do not share in true felicity and free choice."[4] They do not "contemplate the order of things," they do not "deliberate about moral excellence," they do not "deliberate together about the common

3. Oakeshott, *Voice of Liberal Learning*, p. 71. "Education is not learning to do this or that more proficiently; it is acquiring in some measure an understanding of a human condition in which the 'fact of life' is continuously illuminated by a 'quality of life.' It is learning how to be at once an autonomous and civilized subscriber to a human life." And p. 79: in liberal education we do not "attribute an extrinsic 'purpose' to the engagement in which [students] acquire a human character; 'being human,' here, is recognized, not as a means to an end (i.e. living with other human beings), but as a condition for which it is meaningless to ask for a justification in respect of human beings. What else should they be?"

4. Aristotle, *Politics* III, ix, 5, 1280a; Ernest Barker, trans. (Oxford: Oxford University Press, 1946).

good, and decide how to shape and apply the laws."[5] Charles Taylor, in his book *Sources of the Self,* nicely summarizes the tradition in these words:

> The influential ideas of ethical hierarchy exalted the lives of contemplation and participation. We can see a manifestation of the first in the notion that philosophers should not busy themselves with the mere manipulation of things, and hence with the crafts. This was one source of resistance to the new experimental science which Bacon advocated. Scholarly humanism was imbued with this hierarchical notion, which was also linked to a distinction between the true sciences, which admitted of demonstration, and lower forms of knowledge, which could only hope to attain to the "probable," in the sense the words had then, e.g., the forms of knowledge practised by alchemists, astrologers, miners, and some physicians.
>
> We see the second idea returning in early modern times with the various doctrines of civic humanism, first in Italy and later in northern Europe. Life as a mere householder is inferior to one which also involves participation as a citizen. There is a kind of freedom citizens enjoy which others are deprived of. (P. 212)

The Protestant Reformation, and, in particular, the Calvinist branch thereof, represents a radical rejection of this scale of values in which the life of the mind is elevated over that of the citizen, in which both modes of life are elevated over ordinary life, and in which the work of our hands is regarded as having no more than instrumental value. Let me briefly develop this point with the aid of the chapter from Taylor's book which he calls " 'God Loveth Adverbs' " — in my judgment easily the best chapter in the book.

Taylor explains ordinary life as "those aspects of human life concerned with production and reproduction, that is, labour, the making of the things needed for life, and our life as sexual beings, including marriage and the family" (p. 211). It was these, he remarks, that Aristotle classified as life when he invidiously contrasted

5. Quoted phrases taken from Charles Taylor, *Sources of the Self* (Cambridge: Harvard University Press, 1989), pp. 211-12.

life with the good life. And it was these that the Reformers, for the first time in the history of the West, bestowed with inherent and not just instrumental worth — provided they were done to the glory of God and the good of the commonwealth.

> What was previously stigmatized as lower is now exalted as the standard, and the previously higher is convicted of presumption and vanity. . . . [T]his involved a revaluation of professions as well. The lowly artisan and artificer turn out to have contributed more to the advance of science than the leisured philosopher. And indeed, an inherent bent toward social levelling is implicit in the affirmation of ordinary life. The centre of the good life lies now in something which everyone can have a part in, rather than in ranges of activity which only a leisured few can do justice to. (Pp. 213-14)

This affirmation of holy worldliness was most vigorously expressed in the English Puritans. Let me cite some representative passages. John Dod says that

> Whatsoever our callings be, we serve the Lord Christ in them. . . . Though your worke be base, yet it is not a base thing to serve such a master in it. They are the most worthy servants, whatsoever their imploiment bee, that do with most conscionable, and dutifull hearts and minds, serve the Lord, where hee hath placed them, in those works, which hee hath allotted unto them.[6]

William Perkins makes the same point in these words:

> Now if we compare worke to worke, there is a difference betwixt washing of dishes, and preaching of the word of God: but as touching to please God none at all. . . . As the Scriptures call him carnall which is not renewed by the spirit and borne again in Christs flesh and all his workes likewise . . . whatsoever he doth,

6. Quoted in ibid., p. 223. Taylor in turn is quoting from C. H. George and K. George, *The Protestant Mind of the English Reformation: 1570-1640* (Princeton: Princeton University Press, 1961).

though they seem spirituall and after the law of God never so much. So contrariwise he is spirituall which is renewed in Christ, and all his workes which spring from faith seeme they never so grosse . . . yea deedes of matrimonie are pure and spirituall . . . and whatsoever is done within the lawes of God though it be wrought by the body, as the wipings of shoes and such like, howsoever grosse they appeare outwardly, yet are they sanctified.[7]

And here is how Joseph Hall makes the point:

The homeliest service that we doe in an honest calling, though it be but to plow, or digge, if done in obedience, and conscience of God's Commandement, is crowned with an ample reward; whereas the best workes for their kinde (preaching, praying, offering Evangelicall sacrifices) if without respect of God's injunction and glory, are loaded with curses. God loveth adverbs; and cares not how good, but how well.[8]

Thomas Aquinas, in explaining his claim that "the liberal arts excel the mechanical arts," had said that the mechanical arts are "works done by the body, which arts are, in a fashion, servile, inasmuch as the body is in servile subjection to the soul, [whereas] man, as regards his soul, is free *(liber)*" (*S.Th.* I-II, q.3, obj. 3 & ad. 3). Here, by contrast, is a passage from Thomas Adams:

Every one thinkes himselfe Gods sonne: then heare this voyce, Goe my sonne. You have all your vineyards to goe to. Magistrates Goe to the bench to execute judgement and justice. Ministers Goe

---

7. Quoted in Taylor, *Sources of the Self*, p. 224. Compare this passage from Perkins: "Now the works of every calling, when they are performed in an holy manner, are done in faith and obedience, and serve notably for Gods glory, be the calling never so base. . . . The meanenesse of the calling, doth not abase the goodnesse of the worke: for God looketh not at the excellence of the worke, but at the heart of the worker. And the action of a sheepheard in keeping sheep, performed as I have said, in his kind, is as good a worke before God, as is the action of a Judge, in giving sentence or of a Magistrate in ruling, or a Minister in preaching." Quoted in George and George, *Protestant Mind*, p. 138.

8. Quoted in Taylor, *Sources of the Self*, p. 224.

to the Temple, to preach, to pray, to doe the workes of Evangelists. People Goe to your callings, that you may eate the labours of your owne hands: Eye to thy seeing, eare to thy hearing, foote to thy walking, hand to thy working . . . every man to his profession, according to that station, wherein God hath disposed us. . . . The Incitation gives way to the Injunction, worke.[9]

If these passages express the consensus of the tradition — and surely they do — then whatever be the justification that a college in the Reformed tradition of Christianity offers for engaging in the liberal arts, that justification will abjure any suggestion that the life of the mind is nobler than the work of our hands. Conversely, such a college will neither dismiss proposals for educational programs beyond the liberal arts by arguing that such programs are inherently inferior, nor will it admit such programs and then, on the ground of their supposed inferiority, treat them as second-class citizens within the college. A college in the Reformed tradition of Christianity will not look down on the work of our hands. But let us be honest. That is how it ought to be; that is not how it has been. Though for a long time now we have incorporated within our curriculum the work of the hands of our artists, of our musicians, and of our future teachers, there can be no doubt that many of us have looked down on that work.

Obviously no college can be all things to all people; all should avoid even trying. If one does not dismiss educational programs that go beyond the liberal arts on the ground that they are one and all inherently inferior, how does one choose among the options? How does one discriminate?

It is endemic in those engaged in the liberal arts, both at this college and at others, to interpret the appearance of anything beyond the liberal arts in their college as the consequence of the college administration in craven fashion caving in to outside pressures. That is how Michael Oakeshott interprets the fact that what he regards as true schools are now a minority on the educational scene. I do not doubt that college administrations do exhibit a good deal of craven caving in — though I have never been able to bring

9. Quoted in George and George, *Protestant Mind*, pp. 131-32.

myself to believe that they have even a near-monopoly on this failing. Nonetheless, I agree with the assumption of the critics that it is not an appropriate principle of selection for adding programs beyond the liberal arts, to do so when and as one's constituency demands it or one's survival requires it.

What then is an appropriate principle? I suggest that the decision should always be made on the basis of the following two considerations: How important are the goals of the proposed program, and does the program utilize one's strengths as a college with liberal arts at its core? Let me say a word about both the importance and the propriety of the enhancement that I am proposing. Perhaps first, though, I should say once again what that enhancement is. I propose that Calvin College become a place where the Christian community — especially but not only the Reformed branch of that community — does its normative and strategic thinking about (some of) the major social formations of our society, such as business, church, politics, media, medicine, education, law, and art and architecture. Students would be inducted into such thinking. But what I envisage goes beyond the teaching of students. Calvin College would be a place where those already engaged as leaders in those social formations could come apart for a while to do such thinking together — joined by some of us who, though not leaders in those formations, are affected by, and informed about, them.

Why do I think such normative and strategic thinking important? Let me give two reasons. One is a theological reason characteristic of the Reformed tradition; the other, a reason based on analysis of the dynamics of contemporary society. As I suggested earlier, it has been typical of the Reformed tradition of Christianity to regard not only persons as religiously fallen and sinful but social institutions as well; and to regard the Christian as called to work redemptively for the healing of those institutions. It is this combination of convictions that accounts for that reformist and revolutionary impulse of the Calvinist tradition that Michael Walzer explores in his book *The Revolution of the Saints*. In contrast to the conviction of so many Christians in America, the Reformed Christian has never believed that America is a Christian nation and that accordingly our social institutions and formations, though blemished here and there, are fundamentally in accord with God's will.

But neither has he ever agreed with those Christians who hold that our social institutions and formations are fundamentally corrupt and that the duty of the Christian is to withdraw. Normative discrimination is what he has always regarded as the appropriate stance, coupled with the attempt, once the discrimination has been made, to change what is wrong when that proves possible, to keep discontent alive when change proves not possible, and always to be grateful for what is good. In short, to act redemptively. While praying the prayer "Thy kingdom come," to join God's cause of struggling against all that resists and falls short of God's will and longing for creation, thus to acknowledge the rightful, and ultimately effective, rule of Jesus Christ over every square inch of creation.

One serves God and humanity in one's daily occupation; that was ringingly affirmed in those passages I quoted from the Puritans. But one does not serve God and humanity by going into business and then just playing the received role of businessmen, nor by going into medicine and then just playing the received role of physician, nor by going into the academy and then just playing the received role of the academic. For those received roles are religiously fallen — not fallen through and through, but nonetheless fallen. To serve God faithfully and to serve humanity effectively, one has to critique the received role and do what one can to alter the script. There is a great deal of discussion nowadays about medical ethics, legal ethics, business ethics, and so forth. While often participating in such discussions, the Reformed Christian will also want to bracket most of them. For most of them take for granted the present social formations of medicine, law, and business, and then worry about the ethical quandaries that arise for those who act within those formations. The Reformed Christian will want to step back, as Max De Pree did, to ask what is the purpose of business.

My reason of social analysis, for regarding as important such normative and strategic reflection as I am proposing, goes as follows. I think it is true, historically, that the fundamental principles that legitimated and oriented action within the major social institutions and formations here in America were heavily influenced by Christianity. It was always much too simplistic and undiscriminating to say that they just were Christian principles — and that we were, in that way, a Christian country. There were always influences at work in shaping those principles that were alien to Christianity. But Christianity was an important influence; of that there can be no doubt. That is less and less the case, however — for two reasons, as I see it. For one thing, America is now much more religiously diverse than it was at its founding. At its founding, Protestant Christianity enjoyed near hegemony; that is now a thing of the past. But second, the intelligentsia of American society are now much more indifferent and hostile to institutional religion, and especially to institutional Christianity, than is the society at large. And the intelligentsia play a role out of all proportion to their numbers in shaping our major social formations — they especially play a role out of all proportion to their numbers in setting the course of media, education, and the arts.

It follows that an educated and self-consciously Christian voice in the shaping of these social formations is becoming more and more necessary. I judge that the social discontent so evident among many Christians in American society today is due to their intuitive realization that the received principles shaping our major social formations are no longer satisfactory to the Christian. There has been a slippage, and that slippage is now widely perceived. Unless there are educated Christian voices and hands within these formations, that slippage will continue.

Those of us who have been defenders of Christian liberal arts education have of course never believed that what we teach our students is good only for the life of the mind. We have neither thought nor said that only for academics is it of benefit to their professional lives, and that only for their leisure time is it of benefit to those who work with their hands. We have believed, and told all who would listen, that it is of benefit to the physician in her work, to the businessman in his work, to the clergyman in his work, to the lawyer in her work, and so forth. But it has also been characteristic of us to leave in vapors of vagueness what exactly that benefit might be and how exactly it might work. Every now and then we invite back to campus some graduate who has gone on into politics or whatever to testify, at commencement or convocation, about the relevance of his liberal arts education to his present work. But such talks, in my experience, are rather more generous in heat than in light — and in smoke than in heat! I do not myself doubt that there actually is some benefit of the sort claimed — though I would prefer not being asked to pinpoint that benefit.

But a presupposition of my case today is that we can do much better, in developing the normative and strategic reflection I am calling for, than just induct people into the academic disciplines or the cultural tradition, and then send them out on their own. The normative and strategic issues that I have in mind are thick and complex; witness the complexity of what is happening today in American politics! They require sustained thought. A program of liberal arts education is not aimed at providing that sustained thought; it is aimed at something else. And while the liberal education of those immersed in leadership positions in our major social formations certainly does give them some of the fundamental equipment necessary for engaging in that sustained thought, they do not have the time actually to engage in it while on the job. You will all have sensed how extraordinary was the policy of the Herman Miller Company, which I mentioned, to have a reflective retreat of its top executives twice a year. But one day twice a year, though certainly better than nothing, does not take one far. I myself judge that what has led to the sprouting up of think tanks all over New York City, Washington D.C., and the Bay Area, is the felt need for sustained normative and strategic thought about our major social formations, especially that of politics. Those think tanks suffer, in my judgment, from their isolation from the liberal arts. And very few are devoted to developing a Christian voice.

In short, normative and strategic Christian reflection on our major social institutions is an obligation of the Christian community and a need of our society. I judge that there is no better place to cultivate such reflection than in the Christian liberal arts college.

I envisage the day when reflective Christians active in the major social formations of our society look to Calvin College as a place where they can get together on a regular basis, and in the context of worship, Bible study, and recollection of the Christian tradition, engage in normative and strategic reflection on the issues of direction and orientation that confront them. It will be a place where they can safely express their nagging doubts and haunting guilt. It will be a place where they can practice the realization that disagreement is not always evil and consensus is not always all: A place where they can learn the Christian ethos of disagreement in which one honors a person in the midst of disagreeing with her, sometimes even honors her by disagreeing with her. A place where they can learn to own the controversies of the Christian tradition along with its consensus. There will be short-term conferences, longer-term symposia, and study centers. Expectations will be modest but genuine. Realistic idealism will be the mood. Rarely will participants speak of "transforming" American society; they will be content to make a difference. Sometimes not even that will be possible; then they will work to keep discontent alive. For we live in the expectant hope that God will someday take those differences and that discontent and effect the transformation. Fidelity to the God revealed in Jesus Christ, celebration of the glimpses of what is good, and lament for the suffering and waywardness of the world, will be what moves the participants. The liberal arts faculty of the college will be intimately involved. And students, who look forward to working in one or another of these social formations, will see their future before them as I saw before me my future in Christian learning when I was witness to the thought and work of my teachers. They will be inducted into that company of reflective, committed, perplexed, fallible, worshiping men and women who are struggling to think with Christian minds, to feel with Christian hearts, and to work with Christian hands, within the social formations of contemporary America.

> Let the favor of the Lord our God be upon us,
>   and prosper for us the work of our hands —
> O prosper the work of our hands!
>
> (Ps. 90:17)

Contributors

Lionel Basney is Professor of English at Calvin College.

Gaylen J. Byker is President of Calvin College.

Russel Botman is Professor of Theology at the University of the Western Cape.

James D. Bratt is Professor of History at Calvin College.

Susan Van Zanten Gallagher is Professor of English at Seattle Pacific University.

Stephen V. Monsma is Professor of Political Science at Pepperdine University.

Richard J. Mouw is President of Fuller Theological Seminary.

William D. Romanowski is Professor of Communication at Calvin College.

Ronald A. Wells is Professor of History and Director of the Calvin Center for Christian Scholarship at Calvin College.

Nicholas P. Wolterstorff is the Noah Porter Professor of Philosophical Theology at Yale Divinity School.

152